Good Housekeeping™
GRILLING COOKBOOK

Good Housekeeping™
GRILLING COOKBOOK

THE BEST RECIPES YOU'LL EVER TASTE

HEARST BOOKS

A Division of Sterling Publishing Co., Inc.

New York

Good Housekeeping

Ellen Levine	EDITOR IN CHIEF
Susan Westmoreland	FOOD DIRECTOR
Susan Deborah Goldsmith	ASSOCIATE FOOD DIRECTOR
Lisa Brainerd Burge, Sandra Rose Gluck, Gina Miraglia, Wendy Kalen, Sara Reynolds, Lori Perlmutter, Mary Ann Svec, Lisa Troland	RECIPE DEVELOPERS
Delia Hammock	NUTRITION DIRECTOR
Sharon Franke	FOOD APPLIANCES DIRECTOR
Gina Davis	ART DIRECTOR

Produced by Rebus, Inc.

Rodney M. Friedman	PUBLISHER
Sandra Rose Gluck	PROJECT EDITOR
James W. Brown, Jr.	ASSISTANT EDITOR
Timothy Jeffs	ART DIRECTOR
Yoheved Gertz	DESIGN ASSISTANT
Regina A. E. Scudellari	ILLUSTRATOR
Hill Nutrition Associates	NUTRITIONISTS

Photography by Brian Hagiwara, Alan Richardson, Mark Thomas, and Ann Stratton

Front jacket photograph by Mark Thomas
Back jacket photographs by Brian Hagiwara (bottom left, top left, top right) and Mark Thomas (bottom right).

Library Of Congress Cataloging-In-Publication Data
Good Housekeeping grilling cookbook / by the editors of Good Housekeeping.
p. cm.
ISBN 1-58816-027-0
1. Barbecue cookery. I. Good Housekeeping Institute (New York, N.Y.)
TX840.B3 G66 2001   99-058460
641.5'784—dc21   CIP

10 9 8 7 6 5 4 3 2 1

Published by Hearst Books
A Division of Sterling Publishing Co., Inc.
387 Park Avenue South, New York, NY 10016

The Good Housekeeping Cookbook Seal guarantees that the recipes in this cookbook meet the strict standards of the Good Housekeeping Institute, a source of reliable information and a consumer advocate since 1900. Every recipe has been triple-tested for ease, reliability, and great taste.

www.goodhousekeeping.com

Distributed in Canada by Sterling Publishing
C/o Canadian Manda Group, One Atlantic Avenue, Suite 105
Toronto, Ontario, Canada M6K 3E7
Distributed in Australia by Capricorn Link (Australia) Pty. Ltd.
P.O. Box 704, Windsor, NSW 2756 Australia

Printed in China

ISBN 1-58816-027-0

Contents

The way to great grilling

Whether you cook over a shoebox-size hibachi or in a state-of-the-art gas-powered "kettle", you know that grilling imparts an incomparable flavor that no other cooking method can. The intense heat, the savory smoke, and the pleasure of cooking (and eating) outdoors all enhance the natural flavor of top-grade steaks, plump chicken breasts, sparkling seafood, and garden-fresh vegetables. You can even bake breads on the grill.

Before you light the fire, spend a few minutes with these pages to assess your grill and utensils, bone up on techniques and flavor-enhancing tricks, and review safety procedures.

TYPES OF GRILLS

You can cook food over a wood fire built in an open pit, but most people appreciate the convenience of a modern barbecue grill. The most sophisticated grills allow you to adjust the heat by turning a knob, and even the most basic have adjustable racks so that you can place the food at the right distance from the fire.

Charcoal

Fueled by charcoal briquettes (pillow-shaped blocks made from hardwood charcoal) or natural hardwood charcoal chunks, these grills are relatively inexpensive. The simplest is the Japanese-style hibachi, a small cast-iron grill just right for a pocket-size patio. For more ambitious grilling, choose a large covered "kettle" with adjustable vents. In between is the versatile uncovered grill sometimes called a brazier. Look for a charcoal grill made of heavy-gauge metal; the legs should be sturdy and positioned to keep the grill stable.

Gas

Today's popular gas grills, fueled by bottled propane or natural gas, can be as easy to light and control as your kitchen stove. They are available with a variety of options, including electronic ignition, fuel gauge, extra burners (for simmering sauces or side dishes), warming racks, and storage cabinets. Some have porcelain-enameled cooking grids for easy cleaning. Gas grills may be grand enough to cook two dozen burgers at a time, or to smoke a whole turkey. You don't sacrifice that delectable barbecue taste because the firebox of a gas grill contains ceramic "briquettes" or lava rocks (made of natural volcanic rock). Meat juices dripping onto these hot "coals" produce a savory flavor.

Electric

The latest thing in grilling is the electric barbecue. Like gas grills, most electric units have artificial briquettes for authentically smoky flavor; these may be removable, so you can also grill indoors, smoke-free. There are large electric grills to use in the backyard (within reach of a grounded electrical outlet) as well as tabletop models for small families and for all-weather indoor use.

Other equipment

Cooking over hot coals calls for some specialized tools, and there are also optional gadgets to consider for easier grilling of fish, kabobs, etc. Here are the basics, plus some extras.

• **Grill topper** If you often grill delicate foods such as seafood and vegetables, you'll want a grill topper—a perforated metal sheet or mesh screen that provides a nearly smooth surface for grilling. Food is less likely to break up or fall through, and you can virtually "stir-fry" cut-up foods over the coals.

• **Grilling baskets** are another option for delicate or small foods. There are classic fish-shaped baskets (to hold whole fish) as well as square and oblong baskets with long handles to hold kabobs, baby vegetables, or fish fillets. Once the food is inside and the basket is clamped shut, you can turn the entire thing at once—easy!

• **Tongs** Better than a fork for turning foods, because they don't pierce the surface and release juices. Barbecue tongs should have heatproof handles and rounded ends that won't cut into the food.

• **Spatula** Use a long-handled one with a heatproof handle for flipping burgers and moving food around on a grill topper (see page 6).

• **Skewers** Long metal skewers are a must for kabobs. Choose skewers with flat shafts, rather than round ones; food will be less likely to slip or turn as it cooks.

• **Basting brush** A heatproof handle and a long shaft are two definite brush requirements. Natural bristles will stand up to the heat better than synthetic ones.

• **Instant-read thermometer** This handy tool is about the size of a medical thermometer, but made of metal. Insert it in food and the dial at the top will give you a reading in seconds.

• **Grilling mitts** are more serious versions of oven mitts—longer, to protect more of your arm, and better insulated to protect you from higher heat. Heavy suede mitts are excellent.

• **Water spray bottle** The kind used to mist plants, adjusted so that it emits a narrow stream to quash flare-ups.

• **Brass-bristled scrub brush** Use this to clean the grill rack. It helps to remove the rack as soon as you're finished cooking, wrap it in dampened newspaper, and soak the whole thing with a hose. When you unwrap it, burned-on food will be softened. (Another time-saver: Line the firebox with heavy-duty foil before you grill.)

FOR THE FIRE

Gas and electric grills are easy to light; just follow the manufacturer's directions. A charcoal fire requires a little more finesse. Be sure to leave enough time after starting the fire for the coals to burn down to gray ash before you start cooking. Allow 40 minutes to be on the safe side.

Getting started

You don't want to run out of heat before the food is cooked, so start with enough briquettes. Estimate the right amount by spreading an even layer of briquettes over the bottom of the firebox. Before lighting, stack the briquettes into a pyramid to allow air to circulate between them. The following are options to help you get the fire going:

• **Chimney starter** An open-ended metal cylinder with a handle. Place crumpled newspaper in the bottom, top with briquettes, and light the paper through an opening in the bottom. The briquettes will quickly burn to ash-covered readiness.

• **Electric starter** A loop-shaped heating element with a handle, this device is placed in a bed of briquettes; plug it in, and the briquettes will ignite.

GRILLING PORK

Cut	Cook to Temperature	Approximate Cooking Time
Chops (rib or loin), 1" thick	160°F	12-14 minutes
Tenderloin, whole	160°F	15-25 minutes
Tenderloin steaks ¼" thick	160°F	6 minutes

THE PERFECT BURGER

- For juiciness and flavor, use *relatively* lean meat, but not the very leanest. You need a little fat for great burgers.

- Don't overmix when combining meat and other ingredients, and don't squeeze or compress the mixture when shaping patties, or you'll end up with dry, tough burgers.

- To prevent sticking, get the grill good and hot before putting on the burgers.

- Salt after cooking, not before; salt draws out juices.

- Never flatten or score burgers with a spatula as they cook, or you'll lose precious juices.

- For safety's sake, cook thoroughly, until just a trace of pink remains in the center (160°F). Burgers don't have to be well-done, but they should not be rare.

- Keep ground beef refrigerated up to 2 days in its supermarket wrap. For longer storage, rewrap in freezer wrap and freeze; use within 3 months.

- **Self-starting briquettes** are impregnated with starter fluid. A match will ignite them immediately. Don't add them to a fire that's already hot.

- **Liquid fire starter** Saturate briquettes with the liquid, then let stand for a minute before lighting. If you wait until the coals are ready for proper cooking (see "Fine-tuning" below), the fluid will have burned off and will not affect the flavor of the food. Never add liquid starter to a fire that's already burning, or to hot coals: a spark could ignite the whole can.

- **Solid fire starter** Place these waxy-looking cubes in the firebox, pile briquettes on top, and light. They're safer to handle than liquid starter.

Fine tuning

You'll know the coals are ready when they are about 80 percent ashy gray (at night, you'll see them glow red). To test the heat, hold your palm above the coals at cooking height (about 6 inches): If the fire is **low** (above 200°F), you'll be able to keep your hand there for 5 to 6 seconds. If you can bear the heat for 4 to 5 seconds, the fire is **moderate** (above 300°F). If you can hold your palm over the fire for just 2 to 3 seconds, the fire is **hot** (above 375°F).

Tapping the coals will remove their ash cover and make the fire hotter. Pushing the coals together intensifies the heat, while spreading them apart decreases it. Opening the vents on a covered grill increases the temperature, and partially closing the vents lowers the heat.

SAFETY TIPS

- Except for grills intended to be used indoors, always cook in the open air. You're safe under a shelter, such as a carport, or in the doorway of a garage (place the grill very close to the open door), but never use a charcoal or gas grill in a closed building or room: The burning coals will consume the oxygen and fill the room with carbon monoxide, with possibly fatal results.
- Have a bucket of sand or water near the grill in case the fire gets out of hand.
- Never add liquid fire starter to an existing fire. The stream of fluid can ignite, and the can could explode.
- Keep an eye on the grill at all times, especially when children and/or pets are on the scene.
- Don't wear scarves or clothing with loose, billowy sleeves, or fringes, when cooking over coals.

• If the fire flares up or food catches fire, raise the rack and spread the coals apart. If necessary, squirt the fire with water from a spray bottle.

• If you want to coat the grill rack with nonstick cooking spray, do so while the rack is cool, and at a good distance from the grill.

MARINADES, ETC.

When food is to be cooked by intense dry heat—as in grilling—marinating and basting helps keep it moist. Although the smoky taste of grilled food is naturally delicious, marinades and seasoning rubs (their dry counterparts) can add an extra dimension of flavor. Marinades often have an acidic component—vinegar, wine, yogurt—which penetrates the surface to a depth of ½ inch or so, thus tenderizing meat (if only slightly) and infusing it with flavor.

Here's the easiest way to marinate: Mix the marinade ingredients in a heavy-duty zip-tight plastic bag, add the food, and seal the bag, pressing out most of the air. Put the bag on a platter to catch leaks or condensation. When marinating meat, poultry, and seafood for more than 30 minutes—or if it's a very warm day—place the bag in the refrigerator. Turn it occasionally to redistribute the marinade. If you're not using a plastic bag, place the food in a noncorrosive bowl or pan (glass, ceramic, stainless steel, or enamel) and cover it.

Delicate foods, such as seafood and boneless chicken breasts, can benefit from marinating just 15 minutes, and should not be left much longer (especially in an acid marinade) or they will begin to turn mushy. Large cuts of beef and pork, and substantial bone-in chicken parts should be marinated for at least an hour, but no more than 24 hours.

A marinade can be brushed onto food as it grills, but since the liquid has been in contact with raw meat, it must be thoroughly cooked before you eat it. Stop basting 10 minutes before the food is done, or the marinade will not have sufficient time to cook. If you plan to serve a marinade as a sauce, you must boil it for at least 1 minute. Discard any leftover marinade; it cannot be reused.

Seasoning rubs are combinations of spices, dried herbs, salt, and, sometimes, moist ingredients such as mustard, oil, or pureed fresh herbs. The mixture is rubbed onto the food before grilling. If possible, apply the rub an hour or two in advance for maximum flavor. A seasoning rub can be used on its own, or complemented with a similarly seasoned sauce.

Basting sauces, including bottled barbecue sauce, should be thick enough to adhere to food as it cooks. Sweet sauces, made with liberal amounts of honey, molasses, or sugar, are likely to burn, so wait until the last 15 minutes of cooking time before brushing them on.

GRILLING BEEF

Cut	Cook to Temperature*	Approximate Cooking Time
Steaks (porterhouse, T-bone, sirloin, rib-eye, top round):		
¾" thick	145°F	6-8 minutes
1" thick	145°F	11-14 minutes
Steaks (flank or skirt)	145°F	15-20 minutes
Tenderloin, whole	135°F	30-40 minutes
Burgers, 1" thick	160°F	10-12 minutes

*FOR MEDIUM-RARE

FLAVORING THE FIRE

In addition to seasoning the food you'll be grilling, you can also flavor the fire itself, or, more specifically, the smoke that rises from it. This works best in a covered grill, which holds in the smoke. Aromatic woods, such as mesquite or hickory, are well-known for the tang they add to grilled meats. Herbs, spices, and other cooking ingredients add their own flavors.

Grilling woods are sold in chunks or chips to be tossed onto a charcoal fire or gas grill. You want the wood to smoke slowly, not burn quickly, so soak it in water before adding it to the coals. Chips require about half an hour of soaking; larger chunks should be soaked for up to two hours. Suit the wood to the food: Use oak and mesquite, which are strongly flavored, for cooking beef and pork; their smoke can overpower fish and poultry. Hickory's sweetness is well suited to turkey, chicken, and pork. Fruitwoods, such as apple and cherry, are mild enough to use with chicken and seafood. If using chunks of wood, add them to the fire from the start; place chips on the coals later in the cooking process.

Dried grapevines give off a subtly wine flavor, and corncobs (dried for a few days after you've cut off the kernels) produce a hickory-like smoke. Partially cracked nuts in the shell, soaked for 15 minutes or so, release their flavors when heated in the coals.

Whole spices, and fresh or dried herbs, can be placed on the fire to complement the seasonings in a marinade or rub. Soak them for about 30 minutes before using. Fennel is traditional for grilling fish, while rosemary, dill, thyme, bay leaves, and cilantro are other options. Experiment with other smoke flavorings, such as whole cinnamon sticks or cloves, strips of orange or lemon peel, and whole garlic cloves.

GRILLING POULTRY

Cut	Cook to Temperature	Approximate Cooking Time
Legs, bone-in	175°F	35-40 minutes
Thighs, bone-in	175°F	12-15 minutes
Thighs, boneless	175°F	10-12 minutes
Breasts, bone-in	175°F	30-35 minutes
Breasts, boneless	175°F	10-12 minutes
Cornish game hens, halved	175°F	35-45 minutes

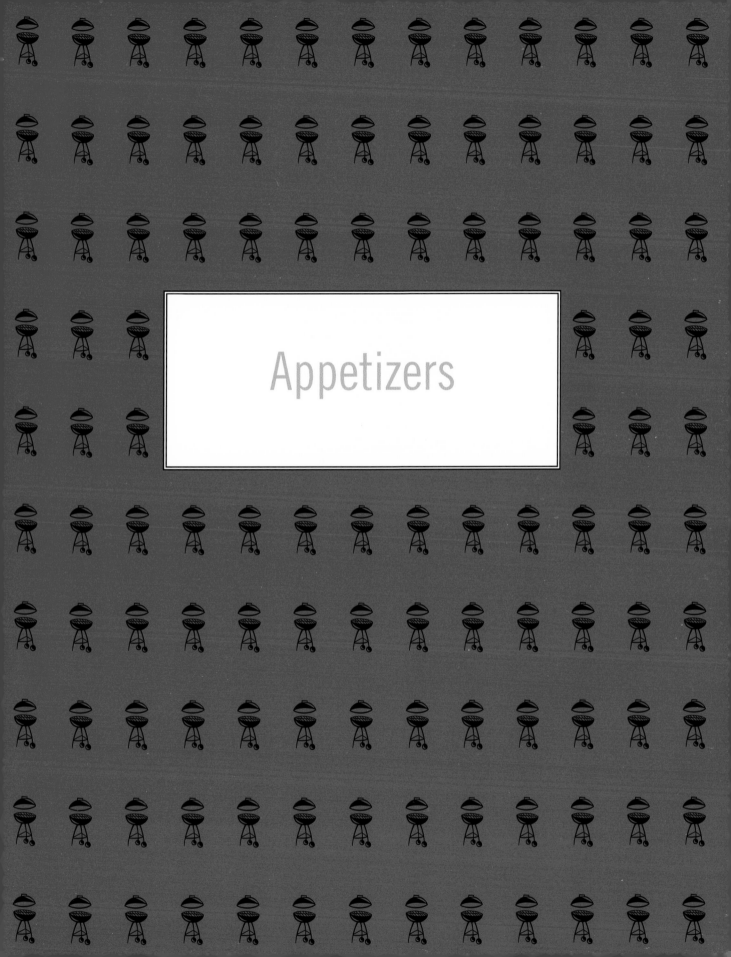

Appetizers

Grilled Pizza

Quick-rise yeast gets mixed right in with the flour and salt and needs no proofing. Grilling pizza
gives it a smoky flavor not unlike that from a wood-burning oven. If you like, grill onions, peppers, and sausages
and let guests personalize their own pizzas.

PREP: 15 MINUTES PLUS RESTING TIME   GRILL: 5 TO 10 MINUTES

2 cups all-purpose flour

1 package quick-rise yeast

¾ teaspoon salt

¾ cup hot water (120° to 130°F)

2 teaspoons plus 2 tablespoons olive oil

8 ounces fresh mozzarella cheese, thinly sliced

12 fresh basil leaves

2 small ripe tomatoes, thinly sliced

Salt

Coarsely ground black pepper

1 Prepare outdoor grill. In large bowl, combine flour, yeast, and salt. Stir in hot water and 2 teaspoons of olive oil until blended and dough comes away from side of bowl. Turn onto lightly floured surface; knead 5 minutes.

2 Shape dough into two 10-inch rounds or four 6-inch rounds. Cover with plastic wrap; let rest 15 minutes.

3 Place rounds on grill rack; grill over medium heat 2 to 5 minutes, until underside turns golden and grill marks appear. With tongs, turn rounds. Brush lightly with some of remaining olive oil. Top with mozzarella, then basil and tomato slices. Grill 3 to 5 minutes longer, until cheese begins to melt. Transfer pizzas to plates. Drizzle with remaining olive oil; sprinkle with salt and pepper.   *Makes 12 servings*

EACH SERVING: About 170 calories, 7 g protein, 17 g carbohydrate, 8 g total fat (3 g saturated), 1 g fiber, 17 mg cholesterol, 225 mg sodium

TIP
No time to make your own dough? Frozen bread dough from the supermarket or pizza dough purchased from your local pizza parlor is a great stand-in for homemade dough. Follow the thawing directions on the package if using frozen dough.

Grilled Flatbread

PREP: 15 MINUTES PLUS RISING   GRILL: 5 MINUTES EACH

1 In large bowl, combine yeast, sugar, and ¼ cup warm water. Let stand until yeast mixture foams, about 5 minutes. Stir in 1½ cups flour, 2 tablespoons olive oil, salt, and remaining 1 cup warm water until combined. With spoon, gradually stir in 2 cups flour. With floured hand, knead mixture in bowl to combine.

2 Turn dough onto lightly floured surface. Knead 10 minutes, until smooth and elastic, working in more flour (about ½ cup) if necessary.

3 Shape into a ball and place in greased large bowl, turning dough over to grease top. Cover and let rise in warm place (80° to 85°F) until doubled, about 1 hour.

4 Punch down dough. Turn dough onto lightly floured surface. Cover; let rest 15 minutes.

5 Prepare grill. Shape dough into 4 balls. On lightly floured surface, with floured rolling pin, roll 1 dough ball at a time into a 12-inch round about ⅛-inch thick. Place rounds on greased large cookie sheets; lightly brush tops with some remaining olive oil.

6 Place 1 round at a time, greased side down, on grill over medium heat. Grill 2 to 3 minutes, until grill marks appear on underside and dough stiffens (dough may puff slightly). Brush top with some oil. With tongs, turn bread over and grill 2 to 3 minutes longer, until grill marks appear on underside and bread is cooked through. Transfer flatbread to tray; keep warm. Repeat with remaining dough.   *Makes 12 servings*

EACH SERVING: About 200 calories, 5 g protein, 33 g carbohydrate, 5 g total fat (1 g saturated), 1 g fiber, 0 mg cholesterol, 390 mg sodium

1 package active dry yeast
1 teaspoon sugar
1¼ cups warm water (105° to 115°F)
   About 4 cups all-purpose flour
   About 3 tablespoons olive oil
2 teaspoons salt

Flatbread with Salad

Try this salad "pizza" as an alternative to the usual tomato-and-cheese kind. Vary your salad ingredients depending upon what's available, or prepare a variety of salad ingredients and dressings and let guests assemble their own flatbread.

PREP: 20 MINUTES PLUS TIME TO PREPARE FLATBREAD   GRILL: 5 MINUTES PER FLATBREAD

1 Prepare Grilled Flatbread through step 5.

2 About 10 minutes before grilling flatbread, prepare salad topping: In large bowl, with wire whisk, mix olive oil, vinegar, sugar, mustard, salt, and pepper until dressing is blended.

3 Add salad greens, tomatoes, and cucumber to dressing in bowl; toss to coat well. Set salad aside.

4 Grill flatbreads as in step 6 of flatbread recipe.

5 To serve, top each flatbread with about 2 cups salad. Cut each round into quarters.   *Makes 8 servings*

EACH SERVING: About 350 calories, 8 g protein, 54 g carbohydrate, 11 g total fat (2 g saturated), 3 g fiber, 0 mg cholesterol, 680 mg sodium

Grilled Flatbread (page 13)

2 tablespoons extra virgin olive oil

2 tablespoons red wine vinegar

1 teaspoon sugar

1 teaspoon Dijon mustard

¼ teaspoon salt

⅛ teaspoon coarsely ground black pepper

6 cups salad greens, such as radicchio, endive, and arugula, cut into ½-inch pieces

2 ripe medium tomatoes, cut into ½-inch pieces

1 small cucumber, peeled and cut into ½-inch pieces

TIP
The flatbread dough can be prepared up to 24 hours ahead. Prepare dough and rather than letting it rise at room temperature, transfer it to a greased bowl, cover loosely with greased plastic wrap, and refrigerate up to 24 hours. Bring the dough to room temperature before proceeding with the recipe.

Grilled Pitas with Caramelized Onions & Goat Cheese

Long, slow cooking of onions makes them especially sweet. The onions can be cooked up 3 days in advance—just bring them to room temperature before spooning over the goat cheese topping.

PREP: 45 MINUTES   GRILL: 3 MINUTES

4 tablespoons olive oil

2 jumbo onions (1 pound each), coarsely chopped

1 teaspoon sugar

¼ teaspoon salt

¼ teaspoon dried tarragon

¼ teaspoon dried thyme

4 (6-inch) pitas, sliced horizontally in half

6 to 7 ounces soft goat cheese, crumbled

1 tablespoon chopped fresh parsley leaves

1 In nonstick 12-inch skillet, heat 2 tablespoons oil over medium heat. Add onions, sugar, and salt, and cook 15 minutes, or until very soft, stirring frequently. Reduce heat to medium-low and cook 20 minutes longer, or until onions are golden brown, stirring frequently.

2 Prepare grill. In cup, stir remaining 2 tablespoons oil with tarragon and thyme. Brush cut sides of pitas with herb mixture; spread with goat cheese, then top with caramelized onions.

3 Place pitas, topping side up, on grill over low heat, and cook 3 minutes, or until bottoms are crisp and topping is heated through. Sprinkle with parsley and cut each pita into 4 wedges to serve.   *Makes 8 servings*

EACH SERVING: About 245 calories, 8 g protein, 27 g carbohydrate, 12 g total fat (4 g saturated), 2 g fiber, 10 mg cholesterol, 310 mg sodium

TIP

For a tasty change, try this with whole-wheat pitas, crumbled feta cheese, and snipped dill.

Fired-Up Green-Onion Pancakes

These tempting appetizers are cooked right on the grill for a rustic look and great flavor. If you like, the dough can be prepared through step 4 up to 24 hours ahead, covered loosely with greased plastic wrap, and refrigerated until you're ready to use it. When you're ready, proceed with the recipe.

PREP: 20 MINUTES PLUS RISING   GRILL: 5 MINUTES PER BATCH

1¼ cups warm water (105° to 115°F)

1 package active dry yeast

1 teaspoon sugar

About 4¼ cups all-purpose flour

12 green onions, chopped (about 1⅓ cups)

1 tablespoon olive oil

1 tablespoon Asian sesame oil

2 teaspoons salt

1 teaspoon coarsely ground black pepper

1 In 2-cup glass measuring cup, mix warm water with yeast and sugar; let stand until yeast mixture foams, about 5 minutes.

2 In large bowl, with wooden spoon, combine 1½ cups flour with green onions, olive oil, sesame oil, salt, pepper, and yeast mixture until blended. Gradually stir in 2½ cups flour. With floured hand, knead mixture in bowl to combine.

3 Turn dough onto lightly floured surface and knead 10 minutes, until smooth and elastic, working in more flour (about ¼ cup) if necessary.

4 Shape into a ball and place in greased large bowl, turning dough over to grease top. Cover and let rise in warm place (80° to 85°F) until doubled, about 1 hour.

5 Punch down dough. Turn dough onto lightly floured surface. Cover and let rest 15 minutes.

6 Shape dough into 6 balls. With hand, firmly press each ball into an 8-inch round. Place 3 rounds on grill over medium heat. Grill 2 to 3 minutes, until grill marks appear on underside and dough stiffens. With tongs, turn rounds over and grill 2 to 3 minutes longer, until grill marks appear on underside and pancakes are cooked through. Repeat with remaining dough. To serve, cut each into 6 wedges   *Makes 18 servings*

EACH SERVING: About 130 calories, 4 g protein, 25 g carbohydrate, 2 g total fat (0 g saturated), 1 g fiber, 0 mg cholesterol, 240 mg sodium

Tuscan White Bean Bruschetta

A first course made with slices of grilled bread and the flavors of sunny Tuscany—the perfect way
to begin an outdoor dinner cooked on the grill. For an attractive presentation, serve a tray of assorted bruschetta
with a bowl of olives and extra olive oil for drizzling.

PREP: 15 MINUTES   GRILL: 10 MINUTES

1 Prepare grill. Cut off ends from loaf of bread; reserve for making bread crumbs another day. Slice loaf diagonally into ½-inch-thick slices.

2 In medium bowl, with fork, lightly mash beans with lemon juice, sage, salt, pepper, 1 tablespoon olive oil, and 2 teaspoons parsley.

3 Place bread slices on grill over medium heat and cook 3 to 5 minutes on each side, until lightly toasted. Rub 1 side of each toast slice with cut side of garlic. Brush with remaining 2 tablespoons olive oil.

4 Just before serving, top toast slices with bean mixture and sprinkle with remaining parsley.   *Makes 8 servings*

EACH SERVING: About 170 calories, 6 g protein, 21 g carbohydrate, 6 g total fat (1 g saturated), 3 g fiber, 0 mg cholesterol, 315 mg sodium

- 1 loaf (8 ounces) Italian bread
- 1 can (15½ to 19 ounces) white kidney beans (cannellini), rinsed and drained
- 1 tablespoon fresh lemon juice
- 1 teaspoon minced fresh sage leaves
- ¼ teaspoon salt
- ⅛ teaspoon coarsely ground black pepper
- 3 tablespoons olive oil
- 3 teaspoons minced fresh parsley leaves
- 2 garlic cloves, each cut in half

TIP
To add extra flavor to the beans, use a fruity, full-bodied extra-virgin olive oil.

Goat Cheese & Tomato Bruschetta

You can make the goat-cheese mixture the day before—but bring it to room temperature before using, and assemble the bruschetta just before serving. For an even lovelier presentation, use a mix of red and yellow tomatoes and sprinkle with snipped chives.

PREP: 15 MINUTES   GRILL: 10 MINUTES

1 loaf (8 ounces) Italian bread

1 package (5½ ounces) soft mild goat cheese, such as Montrachet

1 teaspoon minced fresh oregano leaves

¼ teaspoon coarsely ground black pepper

2 ripe medium tomatoes, seeded and diced

⅛ teaspoon salt

3 tablespoons olive oil

2 teaspoons minced fresh parsley leaves

2 garlic cloves, each cut in half

1 Prepare grill. Cut off ends from loaf of bread; reserve for making bread crumbs another day. Slice loaf diagonally into ½-inch-thick slices.

2 In small bowl, with fork, stir goat cheese, oregano, and pepper until blended. In medium bowl, stir tomatoes with salt, 1 teaspoon olive oil, and 1 teaspoon parsley.

3 Place bread slices on grill over medium heat and cook 3 to 5 minutes on each side, until lightly toasted. Rub 1 side of each toast slice with cut side of garlic. Brush with remaining olive oil.

4 Just before serving, spread goat-cheese mixture on toast and top with tomato mixture. Sprinkle with remaining parsley.   *Makes 8 servings*

EACH SERVING: About 180 calories, 6 g protein, 16 g carbohydrate, 10 g total fat (4 g saturated), 1 g fiber, 9 mg cholesterol, 280 mg sodium

TIP
Want an even simpler preparation? Omit the goat-cheese mixture, add a tablespoon of chopped fresh basil to the tomatoes, and spoon the mixture over the grilled bread.

Portobello & Prosciutto Salad

Thick and meaty portobello mushrooms have a natural affinity for the grill.
They're great in a salad or served alongside a thick, juicy steak. The stems, which are woody, may be
saved and used in soups or stocks, where they'll lend an earthy flavor.

PREP: 30 MINUTES   GRILL: 8 TO 10 MINUTES

2 bunches arugula (about 8 ounces total), tough stems removed

2 tablespoons balsamic vinegar

2 tablespoons olive oil

2 tablespoons minced shallots

2 tablespoons chopped fresh parsley leaves

¼ teaspoon salt

¼ teaspoon coarsely ground black pepper

4 portobello mushrooms (about 1½ pounds), stems discarded

8 ounces thinly sliced prosciutto

½ cup shaved Parmesan curls (1 ounce)

1 Prepare grill. Arrange arugula on platter.

2 In small bowl, mix balsamic vinegar, olive oil, shallots, parsley, salt, and pepper until blended.

3 Place mushrooms, top side up, on grill over medium heat. Brush mushroom tops with 1 tablespoon dressing. Grill 4 minutes. Turn mushrooms and brush with 2 tablespoons dressing. Grill 5 minutes longer, or until tender.

4 Thickly slice mushrooms and arrange on arugula. Spoon remaining dressing over salad. Arrange prosciutto on platter with salad. Top with Parmesan curls. *Makes 4 servings*

EACH SERVING: About 270 calories, 23 g protein, 9 g carbohydrate, 17 g total fat (4 g saturated), 3 g fiber, 51 mg cholesterol, 1320 mg sodium

TIP
Grilled portobellos make great "pizzas." Once the mushrooms have been turned and grilled, top them with shredded mozzarella and continue grilling just until the cheese has melted. Top each with a sprinkling of finely chopped tomato and a sprig of fresh basil.

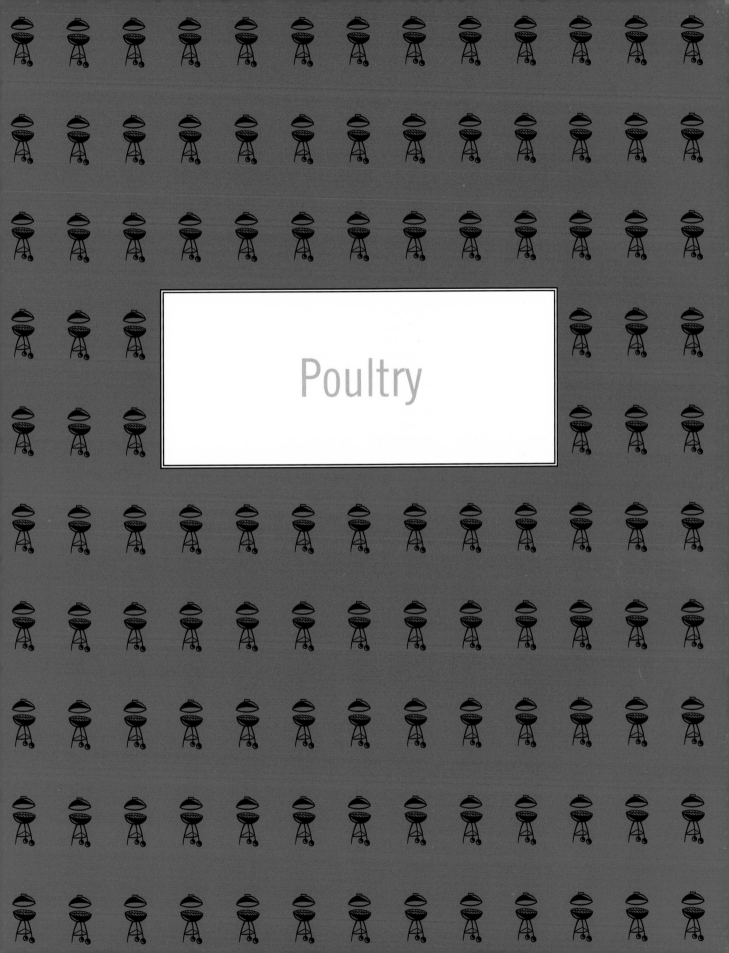

Poultry

All-American BBQ Chicken

Try our sweet and spicy sauce on pork spareribs, too. If you'd prefer, substitute chicken thighs or bone-in breasts for the whole chickens. Wait until the chicken has cooked for 20 minutes before brushing it with sauce and it will become beautifully glazed without burning.

PREP: 60 MINUTES   GRILL: 40 TO 45 MINUTES

2 tablespoons olive oil

1 large onion, chopped

2 cans (15 ounces each) tomato sauce

1 cup red wine vinegar

½ cup light (mild) molasses

¼ cup Worcestershire sauce

⅓ cup packed brown sugar

¾ teaspoon ground red pepper (cayenne)

2 chickens (3½ pounds each), each cut into quarters

1 In 10-inch skillet, heat olive oil over medium heat. Add onion and cook until tender, about 10 minutes. Stir in tomato sauce, vinegar, molasses, Worcestershire, brown sugar, and ground red pepper; heat to boiling over high heat. Reduce heat to medium-low and cook, uncovered, 45 minutes, or until sauce thickens slightly. If not using sauce right away, cover and refrigerate to use within 2 weeks. Reserve 1½ cups sauce to serve with grilled chicken.

2 Prepare grill. Place chicken quarters on grill over medium heat; cook 20 minutes, turning chicken once. Generously brush chicken with some of the remaining barbecue sauce; cook 20 to 25 minutes longer, turning pieces often and brushing with sauce frequently, until juices run clear when chicken is pierced with tip of knife. Serve with reserved sauce. *Makes 8 servings*

EACH SERVING: About 590 calories, 50 g protein, 36 g carbohydrate, 27 g total fat (7 g saturated), 2 g fiber, 154 mg cholesterol, 880 mg sodium

TIP

For a lighter version, remove the skin from the chicken before grilling. Brush the grill with a little oil to prevent sticking and proceed with the recipe.

Mediterranean Chicken Sandwiches

The flavors of the Mediterranean give this sandwich its special zip. Use the olive mayonnaise as a spread for beef or chicken sandwiches as well. For an added touch, stir grated lemon or orange peel into the mayonnaise mixture. For a super chicken salad, cut grilled cutlets into bite-size pieces and toss with the mayonnaise mixture and crisp greens.

PREP: 25 MINUTES   GRILL: 10 TO 12 MINUTES

1 In mortar with pestle, crush fennel seeds with thyme, salt, and pepper. Rub both sides of chicken breasts with fennel-seed mixture; set aside.

2 Prepare grill. In small bowl, mix olives and mayonnaise. Cut bread crosswise into 4 equal pieces, then cut each piece horizontally in half. Spread olive mixture evenly on cut sides of bread; set aside.

3 Place chicken on grill over medium heat and cook 10 to 12 minutes, turning once, until juices run clear when thickest part is pierced with tip of knife. Transfer chicken to cutting board.

4 To assemble sandwiches, slice chicken breasts crosswise into ¼-inch-thick slices. On bottom halves of bread, layer sliced chicken and tomatoes. Replace top halves of bread.   *Makes 4 servings*

EACH SERVING: About 400 calories, 38 g protein, 32 g carbohydrate, 12 g total fat (2 g saturated), 3 g fiber, 86 mg cholesterol, 910 mg sodium

- 1   teaspoon fennel seeds
- ½   teaspoon dried thyme
- ½   teaspoon salt
- ¼   teaspoon coarsely ground black pepper
- 4   medium skinless, boneless chicken-breast halves (about 1¼ pounds)
- ¼   cup Kalamata olives, pitted and minced
- 2   tablespoons mayonnaise
- 1   loaf (8 ounces) Italian bread
- 2   small tomatoes, each cut into 4 slices

TIP
Double the grilled flavor and grill the bread too. Cut bread as directed, then grill pieces for about 1½ minutes per side before spreading with the mayonnaise mixture.

Portuguese Mixed Grill

We've used chorizo instead of the less readily available Portuguese sausage linguiça. Chorizo, a spicy Spanish sausage, is often available in packages of 2 in the meat or deli section of your supermarket. Be sure to purchase fully cooked chorizo.

PREP: 30 MINUTES PLUS MARINATING   GRILL: 25 MINUTES

1 In large bowl, combine vinegar, salt, pepper, 2 tablespoons olive oil, and 1 tablespoon chopped oregano; add chicken thighs, tossing to coat. Refrigerate 30 minutes to marinate.

2 Prepare grill. Meanwhile, cut each red onion into 6 wedges; thread onto 3 metal skewers.

3 Place red-onion skewers on grill over medium heat; brush with remaining 1 tablespoon olive oil. Cook 5 minutes. Place chicken thighs on grill with onions; cook about 20 minutes longer, turning onions and chicken once, until onions are browned and tender and juices run clear when chicken thighs are pierced with tip of knife.

4 About 10 minutes before onions and chicken are done, add chorizo pieces to grill and cook, turning chorizo occasionally, until lightly browned and heated through.

5 To serve, place red-onion skewers on platter with chicken and chorizo. Sprinkle with remaining 1 tablespoon chopped oregano. Serve with olives. Garnish with oregano sprigs. *Makes 6 servings*

EACH SERVING: About 550 calories, 48 g protein, 10 g carbohydrate, 35 g total fat (11 g saturated), 1 g fiber, 187 mg cholesterol, 1,240 mg sodium

- ¼ cup red wine vinegar
- 1 teaspoon salt
- ½ teaspoon coarsely ground black pepper
- 3 tablespoons olive oil
- 2 tablespoons chopped fresh oregano leaves
- 8 large skinless chicken thighs (about 6 ounces each)
- 3 medium red onions
- ¾ pound fully cooked chorizo sausage links, each cut crosswise in half
- ⅔ cup assorted olives such as Kalamata, cracked green, and Picholine (optional)

    Oregano sprigs for garnish

TIP
Serve this flavorful dish with a simple salad of tomato and cucumber chunks tossed with some fresh oregano and a drizzle of olive oil.

Apricot-Ginger Chicken Legs

This quickly-put-together sauce can be served as a dipping sauce as well. If the sauce is too thick to spread, combine all the ingredients in a small saucepan and heat at the edge of the grill until the sauce is spreading consistency. For a change of pace, substitute orange marmalade for the apricot preserves.

PREP: 10 MINUTES   GRILL: 35 MINUTES

2 green onions, chopped

½ cup apricot preserves

⅓ cup ketchup

2 tablespoons cider vinegar

1 tablespoon plus 1 teaspoon grated peeled fresh ginger

1 tablespoon plus 1 teaspoon soy sauce

6 large chicken legs (about 3¾ pounds)

1 Prepare grill. In small bowl, mix green onions, apricot preserves, ketchup, vinegar, ginger, and soy sauce.

2 Place chicken legs on grill over medium heat; cook until golden on both sides, about 10 minutes. Then, to avoid charring, stand chicken legs upright, leaning 1 against the other. Rearrange pieces from time to time and cook until fork-tender and juices run clear when pierced with knife, about 25 minutes longer. During last 10 minutes of cooking, brush chicken legs frequently with apricot mixture.   *Makes 6 servings*

EACH SERVING: About 410 calories, 37 g protein, 22 g carbohydrate, 19 g total fat (5 g saturated), 1 g fiber, 129 mg cholesterol, 520 mg sodium

TIP

If you prefer a smooth sauce, start with ⅔ cup of apricot preserves and push the preserves through a fine-mesh sieve to remove any large chunks.

Flame-Cooked Chicken Saltimbocca

So simple, yet so flavorful, this will quickly become a part of your outdoor repertoire. Remember, cutlets are thin, so make sure you don't overcook them. These would be delicious served between 2 layers of grilled focaccia or our Grilled Flatbread (page 13).

PREP: 15 MINUTES   GRILL: 8 MINUTES

2 tablespoons fresh lemon juice

1 tablespoon olive oil

8 chicken cutlets or skinless, boneless chicken-breast halves with tenderloins removed (2 pounds)

24 large fresh sage leaves

8 thin slices prosciutto (4 ounces)

1 Lightly grease grill. In large bowl, with fork, mix lemon juice and olive oil. Add chicken and toss to coat.

2 Lay 3 sage leaves on each chicken cutlet. Wrap a slice of prosciutto around each cutlet. Grill cutlets 8 minutes, turning once, until juices run clear when thickest part is pierced with tip of knife. Arrange chicken on platter. *Makes 8 servings*

EACH SERVING: About 195 calories, 31 g protein, 1 g carbohydrate, 7 g total fat (2 g saturated), 0 g fiber, 83 mg cholesterol, 410 mg sodium

TIP
If you can't find prosciutto, substitute slices of lean bacon. Serve Horseradish Salsa (page 124) as a tasty accompaniment.

Chicken with Gremolata Salsa

Gremolata, a sprightly combination of parsley, lemon peel, and garlic, is tossed with sun-ripened tomatoes for a full-flavored summer treat. For a change, try grated orange peel instead of the lemon and basil instead of the parsley. If you like, remove chicken skin and brush quarters with 1 tablespoon of oil before cooking to lighten the dish.

PREP: 15 MINUTES   GRILL: ABOUT 40 MINUTES

1 Prepare grill. In small bowl, stir tomatoes, parsley, lemon peel, garlic, olive oil, ½ teaspoon salt, and ¼ teaspoon pepper. Set salsa aside. Makes about 3 cups.

2 Sprinkle chicken with remaining ½ teaspoon salt and ¼ teaspoon pepper.

3 Place chicken on grill over medium heat and cook 20 minutes. Turn chicken over and cook 20 to 25 minutes longer, until juices run clear when thickest part of thigh is pierced with tip of knife.

4 Serve chicken with salsa. Garnish each serving with a grilled green onion if you like.   *Makes 4 servings*

EACH SERVING: About 460 calories, 49 g protein, 6 g carbohydrate, 25 g total fat (7 g saturated), 2 g fiber, 154 mg cholesterol, 740 mg sodium

4 ripe medium tomatoes, diced

2 tablespoons finely chopped fresh parsley leaves

1 teaspoon freshly grated lemon peel

1 small garlic clove, minced

1 teaspoon olive oil

1 teaspoon salt

½ teaspoon coarsely ground black pepper

1 chicken (about 3½ pounds), cut into quarters

   Grilled green onions for garnish (optional)

TIP
Mix up a batch of the lemon-scented tomato salsa to spoon over grilled zucchini, eggplant, or a mixture of vegetables.

Grilled Chicken Cutlets with Tomato-Olive Relish

Our tasty no-cook relish was inspired by Italian puttanesca sauce. Serve the cutlets with a crisp green vegetable or a side dish of Mediterranean Grilled Eggplant & Summer Squash (page 118).

PREP: 15 MINUTES   GRILL: 10 TO 12 MINUTES

1 In small bowl, mix tomatoes, olives, red onion, capers, vinegar, and 1 teaspoon olive oil; set aside.

2 Prepare grill. In medium bowl, toss chicken breasts with salt, pepper, and remaining 2 teaspoons olive oil to coat.

3 Place chicken on grill over medium heat. Cook chicken 5 to 6 minutes per side, or until juices run clear when thickest part is pierced with tip of knife, turning once. Serve chicken topped with tomato-olive relish and garnish with olives.   *Makes 4 servings*

EACH SERVING: About 200 calories, 27 g protein, 5 g carbohydrate, 7 g total fat (1 g saturated), 1 g fiber, 66 mg cholesterol, 565 mg sodium

2 ripe medium tomatoes, diced

¼ cup Kalamata olives, pitted and coarsely chopped

2 tablespoons minced red onion

2 tablespoons drained capers

1 teaspoon red wine vinegar

3 teaspoons olive oil

4 small skinless, boneless chicken-breast halves (about 1 pound)

¼ teaspoon salt

¼ teaspoon coarsely ground black pepper

Kalamata olives for garnish

TIP
If you'd like, double the tomato-olive mixture and toss half with 8 ounces of cooked corkscrew pasta. Serve the pasta at room temperature alongside the chicken.

Grilled Chicken & Mango Salad

The velvety texture of mango, paired with the crunch of cucumber and the sweet, smoky flavor of grilled corn, makes this salad particularly appealing. If mangoes are not available, try firm, ripe nectarines, plums, peaches or a combination of all three.

PREP: 30 MINUTES   GRILL: 15 MINUTES

¼ cup olive oil

¼ cup seasoned rice vinegar

¾ teaspoon salt

¼ teaspoon ground red pepper (cayenne)

4 medium chicken thighs (1½ pounds with bones)

1 large shallot, minced

¼ cup loosely packed fresh cilantro leaves, chopped

1 tablespoon chopped fresh mint leaves

1 tablespoon minced peeled fresh ginger

½ teaspoon freshly grated lemon peel

1 mango, peeled and cut into ¼-inch pieces

1 Kirby cucumber (about 5 ounces), cut into ¼-inch pieces

4 ears corn, husks and silk removed

10 cups mixed baby greens (5 ounces)

1 In medium bowl, with wire whisk or fork, mix olive oil, vinegar, salt, and ground red pepper. Spoon 3 tablespoons oil mixture into pie plate. Add chicken to mixture in pie plate; turn to coat. Marinate 15 minutes at room temperature or 30 minutes in the refrigerator, turning once.

2 Prepare grill. Meanwhile, into oil mixture in bowl, stir shallot, cilantro, mint, ginger, and lemon peel. Stir in mango and cucumber; set aside.

3 Place chicken on grill over medium heat; discard marinade in pie plate. Cook chicken 12 to 15 minutes, until juices run clear when thickest part is pierced with tip of knife, turning once. At the same time, grill corn 10 to 15 minutes, turning often, until lightly browned. Transfer chicken and corn to plate; cool slightly, until easy to handle.

4 When cool, remove and discard skin and bones from chicken thighs. With fingers, pull meat into shreds. With sharp knife, cut kernels from corncobs. Toss chicken and corn with mango mixture.

5 To serve, place greens on 4 dinner plates; top with corn mixture.

Makes 4 servings

EACH SERVING: About 385 calories, 23 g protein, 37 g carbohydrate, 18 g total fat (4 g saturated), 5 g fiber, 70 mg cholesterol, 655 mg sodium

Turkey on the Grill

This easy method yields tender meat, crispy skin, and a smoky flavor. There's no turning or basting, and little fuss. (Note: When turkey is cooked on a covered grill, there may be a narrow, rosy-pink band of meat just under the skin. This doesn't mean the meat is undercooked—it's a result of charcoal combustion reacting with the pigment in the meat.)

PREP: 15 MINUTES   GRILL: 2¼ TO 3 HOURS

1 Prepare coals: In bottom of covered charcoal grill, with vents open and grill uncovered, ignite 60 charcoal briquettes (not self-starting). Allow briquettes to burn 30 minutes, or until coals are covered with a thin coating of gray ash. Push briquettes to 2 sides of grill; place sturdy disposable foil pan (about 13" by 9" by 2") between coals.

2 Rinse turkey with cold running water; drain well. Fasten neck skin to back with skewers. With breast side up, fold wings under back of turkey. Tie legs and tail together with string, or push drumsticks under band of skin. In cup, mix remaining ingredients. Rub over turkey.

3 Place turkey, breast side up, on cooking grate directly over foil pan (to catch drips). Cover grill and roast turkey 2¼ to 3 hours, adding 8 to 9 more briquettes to each side of pan every hour to maintain a grill temperature of 325°F on oven or grill thermometer. Cook until thigh temperature reaches 180° to 185°F on meat thermometer and juices run clear when thickest part of thigh is pierced with tip of knife.

4 Place on warm platter; let stand 15 minutes to set juices for easier carving. Carefully remove drip pan from grill. If you like, skim fat from drippings and serve drippings along with turkey.   *Makes 12 servings*

EACH SERVING: About 535 calories, 73 g protein, 0 g carbohydrate, 25 g total fat (7 g saturated), 0 g fiber, 212 mg cholesterol, 380 mg sodium

1   fresh or frozen (thawed) turkey (12 pounds), giblets and neck removed

2   tablespoons vegetable oil

2   teaspoons dried sage leaves

2   teaspoons dried thyme

2   teaspoons salt

½   teaspoon coarsely ground black pepper

TIP
Be sure the thermometer is not touching the bone when testing the turkey for doneness. Bone conducts heat and will register a higher temperature than the meat itself.

Grilled Basil Chicken & Baby Greens

Fragrant basil leaves turn everyday chicken breasts into something special. Slicing basil can be
a breeze: Stack the leaves one on top of the other, then roll them up into a compact cylinder. Use a sharp
knife to thinly slice the whole stack of leaves at once.

PREP: 20 MINUTES   GRILL: 25 MINUTES

1　large bunch basil

4　medium chicken-breast halves

¾　teaspoon salt

¼　teaspoon coarsely ground black
　　pepper

3　ripe medium tomatoes, chopped

¼　cup olive oil

2　tablespoons white wine vinegar

2　teaspoons freshly grated lemon
　　peel

½　teaspoon Dijon mustard

4　ounces mixed baby greens (8
　　cups) or sliced romaine lettuce
　　leaves

　　Lemon-peel slivers for garnish

1 From bunch of basil, reserve 8 large leaves, and measure 1 cup
loosely packed small leaves. Finely slice enough of the remaining
leaves to equal ½ cup loosely packed. Cover and refrigerate small and
sliced leaves.

2 Prepare grill. Place 2 reserved large basil leaves under skin of each
chicken-breast half. Sprinkle chicken breasts with ¼ teaspoon salt and
⅛ teaspoon pepper. Place chicken, skin side up, on grill over medium
heat. Grill chicken 25 minutes, or until juices run clear when thickest
part of breast is pierced with tip of knife and skin is brown and crisp,
turning chicken once.

3 Meanwhile, in small bowl, stir tomatoes, olive oil, vinegar, lemon
peel, mustard, remaining ½ teaspoon salt, and remaining ⅛ teaspoon
pepper.

4 To serve, in large bowl, toss baby greens with small basil leaves. Stir
sliced basil leaves into tomato mixture. Toss greens with ½ cup tomato
mixture. Arrange greens on 4 dinner plates; top with chicken breasts.
Spoon remaining tomato mixture over breasts. Garnish with lemon-peel
slivers.   *Makes 4 servings*

EACH SERVING: About 340 calories, 31 g protein, 6 g carbohydrate, 22 g total fat
(5 g saturated), 2 g fiber, 83 mg cholesterol, 490 mg sodium

Cornish Hens with Ginger-Plum Glaze

The hens are cut in half for fast, even cooking, then brushed with a gingery plum jam. Glazed plum halves are grilled right alongside. Tossed in the jam-ginger mixture and grilled by themselves, the glazed plums would be a fine finish to any summer barbecue.

PREP: 25 MINUTES   GRILL: ABOUT 30 MINUTES

⅔ cup plum jam or preserves

3 teaspoons grated peeled fresh ginger

4 large plums, each cut in half

2 Cornish hens (about 1¾ pounds each)

2 tablespoons reduced-sodium soy sauce

1 teaspoon Chinese five-spice powder

¾ teaspoon salt

¼ teaspoon coarsely ground black pepper

2 small garlic cloves, crushed with garlic press

1 In 1-quart saucepan, heat plum jam and 1 teaspoon ginger over low heat, stirring, 1 to 2 minutes, until jam melts. Spoon 2 tablespoons plum glaze into medium bowl; add plums and toss to coat. Set glaze aside.

2 Prepare grill. Remove giblets and necks from hens; freeze to use in soup another day. With kitchen shears, cut each hen in half. Pat hens dry with paper towels.

3 In small bowl, mix remaining 2 teaspoons ginger with soy sauce, Chinese five-spice powder, salt, pepper, and garlic. Brush mixture on hen halves.

4 Place hen halves, skin side down, on grill over medium heat and cook 15 minutes, turning once. Brush skin side of hens with plum glaze from saucepan; turn hens over and cook 5 minutes. Brush hens with remaining glaze; turn over and cook 10 minutes longer, or until juices run clear when thickest part of thigh is pierced with tip of knife and hens are golden.

5 Just before hens are done, place plums on grill and cook about 6 minutes, or until plums are hot and lightly browned, turning once.

Makes 4 servings

EACH SERVING: About 620 calories, 39 g protein, 47 g carbohydrate, 31 g total fat (8 g saturated), 3 g fiber, 219 mg cholesterol, 920 mg sodium

Baby Spinach with Nectarines & Grilled Chicken

Prepare this colorful salad with any ripe summer fruit. Try substituting a soft, creamy goat cheese for the feta and add a topping of chopped toasted pecans for an extra treat.

PREP: 25 MINUTES   GRILL: ABOUT 15 MINUTES

1 Prepare grill. Rub chicken with thyme, ½ teaspoon salt, and ¼ teaspoon pepper. Place chicken on grill over medium heat. Cook chicken about 7 minutes per side, or until juices run clear when thickest part is pierced with tip of knife, turning once. Transfer chicken to cutting board; cool until easy to handle.

2 Meanwhile, in large bowl, with wire whisk, mix olive oil, vinegar, mustard, shallot, remaining ¼ teaspoon salt, and ¼ teaspoon pepper. Stir in nectarines and cucumber.

3 To serve, cut chicken into ½-inch-thick slices. Toss spinach with nectarine mixture. Arrange salad on 4 plates; top with feta and sliced chicken.   *Makes 4 servings*

EACH SERVING: About 290 calories, 31 g protein, 15 g carbohydrate, 12 g total fat (3 g saturated), 4 g fiber, 78 mg cholesterol, 730 mg sodium

- 4 small skinless, boneless chicken-breast halves (about 1 pound)
- 1 teaspoon fresh thyme leaves
- ¾ teaspoon salt
- ½ teaspoon coarsely ground black pepper
- 2 tablespoons olive oil
- 1 tablespoon balsamic vinegar
- ½ teaspoon Dijon mustard
- 1 shallot, minced
- 2 large ripe nectarines, pitted and sliced
- ½ English (seedless) cucumber, cut lengthwise in half, then thinly sliced crosswise
- 8 ounces baby spinach
- 2 ounces feta cheese, crumbled

TIP
Baby spinach, with its soft, delicate leaves, is often sold in prepackaged bags. If you can't find baby spinach, look for spinach with smooth, rather than ruffled, leaves and tender stems.

39   Poultry

Citrus Sage Chicken

You can double the citrus-sage mixture and reserve half of it. Serve the reserved mixture as a sauce to spoon over the grilled chicken. Fresh sage leaves have an earthy flavor. If you have extra citrus peels and sage and are using a charcoal grill, toss them onto the charcoal to flavor the smoke.

PREP: 25 MINUTES PLUS MARINATING   GRILL: 30 TO 35 MINUTES

2 large oranges

2 large lemons

¼ cup chopped fresh sage leaves

2 tablespoons olive oil

2 teaspoons salt

¾ teaspoon coarsely ground black pepper

2 chickens (3½ pounds each), each cut into eighths, skin removed

Fresh sage leaves for garnish

1 Grate 1 tablespoon peel and squeeze 3 tablespoons juice from oranges. Grate 1 tablespoon peel and squeeze 3 tablespoons juice from lemons.

2 In large bowl, with wire whisk or fork, combine orange and lemon peels, orange and lemon juices, sage, olive oil, salt, and pepper. Add chicken, turning to coat. Cover and refrigerate 2 hours, turning pieces 3 or 4 times.

3 Prepare grill. Place chicken on grill over medium heat. Cook chicken 20 minutes. Turn chicken and cook 10 to 15 minutes longer, until juices run clear when chicken is pierced with tip of knife.

4 Place chicken in large serving dish; garnish with sage leaves.

Makes 8 servings

EACH SERVING: About 455 calories, 48 g protein, 2 g carbohydrate, 27 g total fat (7 g saturated), 0 g fiber, 154 mg cholesterol, 725 mg sodium

TIP
Try this citrus, sage, and olive oil blend as a simple seasoning for veal chops or pork as well as chicken.

Chicken & Beef Saté

For a festive outdoor buffet, prepare several different salads and a large bowl of rice to serve alongside the saté. Be sure to soak the wooden skewers for at least 20 minutes so they don't burn when you put them on the grill. The saté may also be served as an appetizer.

PREP: 45 MINUTES PLUS MARINATING GRILL: 3 TO 7 MINUTES PER BATCH

1 Slice chicken cutlets lengthwise into ¾-inch-wide strips; place in medium bowl. Holding knife almost parallel to work surface, slice steak crosswise into thin strips; place in another bowl.

2 From limes, grate 2 teaspoons peel and squeeze 2 tablespoons juice. In small bowl, with fork, mix lime peel, lime juice, ¼ cup soy sauce, ginger, sugar, and garlic. Stir half of soy-sauce mixture into chicken. Stir remaining soy-sauce mixture into beef. Cover and refrigerate both bowls 30 minutes to marinate chicken and beef.

3 Soak wooden skewers in water 20 minutes. Meanwhile, in medium bowl, with wire whisk or fork, mix peanut butter, ¼ cup very hot tap water, rice vinegar, remaining 1 tablespoon soy sauce, molasses, and crushed red pepper until smooth.

4 Prepare Cucumber Relish.

5 Prepare grill. Thread chicken strips and beef strips separately on wooden skewers, accordion-style.

6 Grill chicken and beef strips over medium heat 3 to 7 minutes, turning once, until just cooked through. Serve with peanut sauce and Cucumber Relish. *Makes 6 servings*

EACH SERVING: About 370 calories, 39 g protein, 11 g carbohydrate, 19 g total fat (5 g saturated), 1 g fiber, 101 mg cholesterol, 920 mg sodium

1 pound chicken-breast cutlets
1 boneless beef top sirloin steak, 1 inch thick (about 1¼ pounds)
2 large limes
¼ cup plus 1 tablespoon soy sauce
1 tablespoon grated peeled fresh ginger
2 teaspoons sugar
2 garlic cloves, crushed with garlic press
24 (10-inch) wooden skewers
¼ cup creamy peanut butter
4 teaspoons seasoned rice vinegar
1 tablespoon light (mild) molasses
⅛ teaspoon crushed red pepper
Cucumber Relish (page 122)

TIP
To prevent wooden skewers from burning, wrap the exposed ends in foil. For variety, try strips of boneless pork loin instead of beef. Cook pork satés about eight minutes or until cooked through, turning once.

Turkey Cutlets, Indian Style

Delicious with a squeeze of fresh lime or with Mango Salsa (page 120) or Pineapple Salsa
(page 123) served alongside. For a festive presentation, set out bowls of yogurt, store-bought mango chutney,
fluffy basmati rice, and chopped fresh cilantro alongside the cutlets.

PREP: 15 MINUTES   GRILL: 5 TO 7 MINUTES

2   large limes
⅓   cup plain low-fat yogurt
1   tablespoon vegetable oil
2   teaspoons minced peeled ginger
1   teaspoon ground cumin
1   teaspoon ground coriander
1   teaspoon salt
1   garlic clove, crushed with garlic
    press
1½ pounds turkey cutlets
    Cilantro sprigs for garnish

1 Prepare grill. From 1 lime, grate 1 teaspoon peel and squeeze 1 tablespoon juice. Cut the remaining lime into wedges; reserve wedges for squeezing juice over cooked cutlets. In large bowl, mix lime peel, lime juice, yogurt, vegetable oil, ginger, cumin, coriander, salt, and garlic until blended.

2 Just before grilling, add turkey cutlets to bowl with yogurt mixture, stirring to coat cutlets. (Do not let cutlets marinate in yogurt mixture; their texture will become mealy.)

3 Place turkey cutlets on grill over medium heat. Cook cutlets 5 to 7 minutes, until they just lose their pink color throughout. Serve with lime wedges. Garnish with cilantro sprigs.   *Makes 6 servings*

EACH SERVING: About 160 calories, 29 g protein, 3 g carbohydrate, 3 g total fat
(1 g saturated), 0 g fiber, 71 mg cholesterol, 450 mg sodium

TIP
Freeze any extra unpeeled fresh ginger, wrapped well in plastic wrap.
It will keep for up to six months.

Poultry   44

Meat

Pastrami-Spiced Flank Steak

Pastrami, a popular New York City deli item, probably came to us via the Romanians, who prepared many of their meats by smoking. Although our pastrami isn't smoked, it is similarly coated with coarse pepper and other aromatic spices. Serve it on sliced rye with a side of coleslaw, deli-style!

PREP: 15 MINUTES PLUS MARINATING   GRILL: ABOUT 15 MINUTES

1   tablespoon coriander seeds

1   tablespoon paprika

1   tablespoon cracked black pepper

2   teaspoons ground ginger

1½ teaspoons salt

1   teaspoon sugar

½   teaspoon crushed red pepper

1   beef flank steak (about 1½ pounds)

3   garlic cloves, crushed with garlic press

12 slices rye bread

    Deli-style mustard

1 In mortar with pestle, crush coriander seeds. In cup, mix coriander, paprika, black pepper, ginger, salt, sugar, and crushed red pepper.

2 Rub both sides of steak with garlic, then pat with spice mixture. Place steak in large zip-tight plastic bag, pressing out excess air. Place bag on plate; refrigerate at least 2 hours, or up to 24 hours.

3 Prepare grill. Remove steak from bag. Place steak on grill over medium heat and cook 13 to 15 minutes for medium-rare, or until desired doneness, turning steak once. Place bread slices on grill over medium heat and toast, without turning, just until grill marks appear on underside of bread.

4 Transfer steak to cutting board. Let stand 10 minutes to allow juices to set for easier slicing. Thinly slice steak across the grain and serve with grilled rye bread and mustard.   *Makes 6 servings*

EACH SERVING: About 380 calories, 33 g protein, 35 g carbohydrate, 12 g total fat (4 g saturated), 0 g fiber, 47 mg cholesterol, 1,015 mg sodium

TIP
Grinding whole spices in a mortar and pestle releases their flavorful oils, which makes the steak even tastier.

Spice-Rubbed Beef Tenderloin

Fennel seeds, with their licorice-like flavor, are similar to anise seeds, but not quite as sweet. Make a double batch of this rub, store it in a cool, dry place out of the sunlight and use it the next time you're grilling pork chops, pork tenderloin, or a leg of lamb.

PREP: 10 MINUTES   GRILL: 30 TO 40 MINUTES

1   tablespoon fennel seeds

2   teaspoons salt

½   teaspoon ground ginger

½   teaspoon crushed red pepper

1   beef tenderloin roast (about 2½ pounds)

1 In mortar with pestle or in zip-tight plastic bag with rolling pin, crush fennel seeds. In small bowl, combine fennel seeds, salt, ginger, and crushed red pepper. With hands, rub spice mixture on beef tenderloin. If you like, place spice-rubbed beef tenderloin in zip-tight plastic bag and refrigerate several hours or overnight before grilling.

2 Prepare a covered grill. Place beef on grill over medium heat. Cover and cook beef, turning occasionally, 30 to 40 minutes for medium-rare, or until desired doneness. Temperature on meat thermometer should be 135°F (internal temperature will go up to 140°F during standing).

3 Remove beef tenderloin to cutting board and let stand 10 minutes to set juices for easier slicing. Slice beef thinly to serve.

Makes 10 servings

EACH SERVING: About 225 calories, 19 g protein, 0 g carbohydrate, 16 g total fat (6 g saturated), 0 g fiber, 66 mg cholesterol, 510 mg sodium

TIP
Ask your butcher to cut this roast from a whole tenderloin for you. The center-cut roast should be 2½ pounds after trimming; the ends make deliciously tender kabobs.

Meat   48

Red-Wine & Rosemary Porterhouse

This robust marinade can season a thick, juicy steak in 15 minutes. Marinate for up to 1 hour for more intense flavor. It's also good on lamb, pork, or poultry. Serve with Lemon-Garlic Potato Packet (page 112) and Crumb-Topped Tomatoes (page 104).

PREP: 10 MINUTES PLUS MARINATING   GRILL: 15 TO 20 MINUTES

1 In small bowl, stir red wine, Worcestershire, tomato paste, mustard, vinegar, rosemary, and garlic.

2 Place steak in large zip-tight plastic bag. Pour red wine marinade over steak, turning to coat. Seal bag, pressing out excess air. Let stand at room temperature 15 minutes to marinate or refrigerate up to 1 hour, turning once.

3 Prepare grill. Remove steak from bag; discard marinade. Place steak on grill over medium heat and cook 15 to 20 minutes for medium-rare, or until desired doneness, turning steak once.

4 Transfer steak to cutting board. Let stand 10 minutes to allow juices to set for easier slicing. Thinly slice steak and serve with lemon wedges. *Makes 4 servings*

EACH SERVING: About 395 calories, 32 g protein, 1 g carbohydrate, 28 g total fat (11 g saturated), 0 g fiber, 104 mg cholesterol, 125 mg sodium

½ cup dry red wine

1 tablespoon Worcestershire sauce

1 tablespoon tomato paste

1 tablespoon Dijon mustard

1 tablespoon balsamic vinegar

1 tablespoon chopped fresh rosemary leaves

1 large garlic clove, crushed with garlic press

1 beef porterhouse or T-bone steak, 1½ inches thick (about 1½ pounds)

1 lemon, cut into wedges

TIP
For a dry red wine that would work well in this recipe, try a Shiraz, Merlot, Chianti or Cabernet.

Filet Mignon with Horseradish Salsa

Juicy steaks taste even better with our flavor-packed salsa. Looking for a new vegetable idea? Try grilling young onions right along with the meat. For an extra-special company dinner, grill portobello mushrooms as you would in Portobello & Prosciutto Salad (page 22) and serve thickly sliced mushrooms along with the meat and salsa.

PREP: 15 MINUTES   GRILL: 10 TO 12 MINUTES

1 Prepare Horseradish Salsa.

2 Prepare grill. In cup, mix pepper, olive oil, salt, thyme, and garlic. Rub pepper mixture all over steaks. Place steaks on grill over medium heat and cook 10 to 12 minutes for medium-rare, or until desired doneness, turning steaks once. Serve steaks with Horseradish Salsa.

Makes 4 servings

EACH SERVING: About 330 calories, 39 g protein, 9 g carbohydrate, 15 g total fat (4 g saturated), 2 g fiber, 89 mg cholesterol, 710 mg sodium

Horseradish Salsa (page 124)

1   teaspoon cracked black pepper

1   teaspoon olive oil

½   teaspoon salt

¼   teaspoon dried thyme

1   garlic clove, crushed with garlic press

4   beef tenderloin steaks (filet mignons), each 1 inch thick (about 6 ounces each)

TIP
This pepper rub also works beautifully with flank steak, skirt steak, or any sirloin cut.

51   Meat

Barbecued Beef Brisket

This rich barbecued brisket can be made well ahead and then finished on an outdoor grill. Slow-cook the meat on the stove top up to 2 days ahead, then glaze with sauce and grill for 20 minutes to heat through. Leftovers, if there are any, can be heated in a little sauce and spooned over crusty rolls.

PREP: 3 HOURS 25 MINUTES   GRILL: 30 MINUTES

1   fresh beef brisket (4½ pounds), trimmed

1   medium onion, cut into quarters

1   large carrot, cut into 1½-inch pieces

1   bay leaf

1   teaspoon whole black peppercorns

¼   teaspoon whole allspice

Chunky BBQ Sauce (page 121)

1 In 8-quart Dutch oven, place brisket, onion, carrot, bay leaf, peppercorns, allspice, and enough water to cover; heat to boiling over high heat. Reduce heat to low; cover and simmer 3 hours, or until meat is fork-tender.

2 Meanwhile, prepare Chunky BBQ Sauce.

3 When brisket is done, transfer to platter. If not serving brisket right away, cover and refrigerate until ready to serve.

4 To serve, prepare grill. Place brisket on grill (preferably one with a cover) over medium heat and cook 10 minutes. Turn brisket over and cook 5 minutes. Spoon 1 cup barbecue sauce on top of brisket and cook 5 minutes longer, or until brisket is heated through. (Do not turn brisket after topping with sauce.) If you like, reheat remaining sauce in small saucepan on grill. Thinly slice brisket across the grain and serve with sauce.   *Makes 12 servings*

EACH SERVING: About 500 calories, 30 g protein, 4 g carbohydrate, 40 g total fat (15 g saturated), 0 g fiber, 117 mg cholesterol, 185 mg sodium

> ### TIP
> Allspice is available in two forms, whole berries or ground. It gets its name from the fact that it tastes like a combination of cloves, cinnamon and nutmeg. Try adding a few whole berries to hot spiced cider.

Chili-Crusted Flank Steak

The combination of chili powder, sugar, and salt gives the beef a sweet and spicy crust. Grilled red onions, lightly charred and tender, would make a nice addition to any meal off the grill. Serve with Campfire Corn with Herbed Butter (page 108) and grilled bread.

PREP: 10 MINUTES   GRILL: ABOUT 20 MINUTES

1 Prepare grill. In cup, mix chili powder, brown sugar, salt, lime juice, and garlic. Rub both sides of steak with chili-powder mixture. In medium bowl, toss red onions with olive oil.

2 Place steak and onions on grill over medium heat. Cook steak 15 to 20 minutes for medium-rare, or until desired doneness, turning steak once. Cook onions about 15 minutes, or until browned and just tender, turning occasionally.

3 Transfer onions and steak to cutting board. Let steak stand 10 minutes to allow juices to set for easier slicing. Thinly slice steak and serve with grilled onions.   *Makes 6 servings*

EACH SERVING: About 270 calories, 24 g protein, 15 g carbohydrate, 13 g total fat (5 g saturated), 3 g fiber, 57 mg cholesterol, 200 mg sodium

2 tablespoons chili powder

1 tablespoon brown sugar

¼ teaspoon salt

2 tablespoons fresh lime juice

1 large garlic clove, crushed with garlic press

1 beef flank steak (about 1½ pounds)

3 large red onions (about 8 ounces each), each cut into 6 wedges

1 tablespoon olive oil

TIP
You can soak wooden skewers in water for 15 minutes, then thread the onion wedges onto the skewers; the wedges won't separate and will be easier to handle.

Jerk Steak Kabobs with Pineapple Salsa

The hot Caribbean coating on the meat is the perfect foil for our cool tropical salsa. Allspice, a berry grown in the Caribbean, has the combined flavors of cinnamon, cloves, and nutmeg. It is available whole or ground; you'll find it on the spice shelf in your supermarket.

PREP: 30 MINUTES PLUS STANDING   GRILL: 8 TO 10 MINUTES

Pineapple Salsa (page 123)

2 green onions, minced

2 tablespoons lime juice

2 tablespoons brown sugar

1 tablespoon Worcestershire sauce

1 tablespoon grated peeled fresh ginger

1 teaspoon vegetable oil

1 teaspoon salt

1 teaspoon dried thyme

1 teaspoon ground allspice

½ teaspoon ground red pepper (cayenne)

1 boneless beef top sirloin steak, 1¼ inches thick (1½ pounds), cut into 1¼-inch cubes

4 long metal skewers

1 Prepare Pineapple Salsa, cover, and refrigerate.

2 Prepare grill. Meanwhile, in large bowl, mix green onions, lime juice, brown sugar, Worcestershire, ginger, oil, salt, thyme, allspice, and ground red pepper. Add steak cubes and toss to coat well; let stand 15 minutes to marinate.

3 Thread steak cubes on skewers. Place skewers on grill over medium heat; cook 8 to 10 minutes for medium-rare, turning occasionally. Serve kabobs with salsa.   *Makes 4 servings*

EACH SERVING: About 375 calories, 34 g protein, 30 g carbohydrate, 13 g total fat (5 g saturated), 4g fiber, 102 mg cholesterol, 790 mg sodium

TIP
Combine the jerk ingredients: green onions, lime juice, brown sugar, Worcestershire, ginger, vegetable oil, salt, thyme, allspice, and ground red pepper; whirl to a smooth paste in the blender. Transfer to a jar, cover, and store in the refrigerator for up to 1 week.

Greek Burgers

Place the pitas on the grill to toast just before the burgers come off the grill. If you'd like, add crumbled feta cheese and chopped ripe tomatoes to the pitas before serving. Serve the burgers with a crisp romaine lettuce salad tossed with a lemony vinaigrette and snipped fresh dill.

PREP: 5 MINUTES   GRILL: 12 MINUTES

1   pound lean ground beef (90%)
¼   cup chopped fresh parsley leaves
1   teaspoon dried mint leaves
½   teaspoon salt
¼   teaspoon coarsely ground black pepper
4   (6-inch) pitas

1 Prepare grill.

2 In medium bowl, combine ground beef, parsley, mint, salt, and pepper just until well blended but not overmixed. Shape into 4 patties, each 1 inch thick, handling meat as little as possible. (Gentle handling is one of the keys to juicy burgers. Use a light hand when shaping patties, so the burgers won't come out compact and dry.)

3 Grill burgers over medium heat for 10 to 12 minutes for medium, or until desired doneness, turning once. Meanwhile, cut off 1 inch across top of each pita. Serve burgers in pitas.   *Makes 4 servings*

EACH SERVING: About 360 calories, 29 g protein, 34 g carbohydrate, 12 g total fat (5 g saturated), 1 g fiber, 70 mg cholesterol, 695 mg sodium

TIP
Before shaping burgers, tuck a chunk of soft, melting cheese such as Fontina, Cheddar or Roquefort into the center and shape the patty around it to make an inside-out cheeseburger.

Meat   56

Steak Fajitas with Guacamole

Spicy skirt steak with onions makes a memorable Tex-Mex meal. A typical piece of skirt steak is long, about 4 inches wide, and ½ inch thick. If you can't find any skirt steak, flank steak is a good alternative. If low-fat flour tortillas are not available, substitute regular tortillas.

PREP: 25 MINUTES   GRILL: 20 MINUTES

1 Prepare Guacamole.

2 In cup, mix chili powder, cumin, salt, and ground red pepper. Rub steak with 2 tablespoons chili-powder mixture; set aside.

3 Prepare grill. In large bowl, toss onions with oil and remaining chili-powder mixture. Layer two 24'' by 18'' sheets heavy-duty foil to make a double thickness. Place onion mixture on center of foil. Bring short ends of foil up and over onions, and fold several times to seal. Fold remaining sides of foil several times to seal in juices.

4 Place foil packet on grill over medium heat. Cook onions 20 minutes, or until tender, turning packet over halfway through cooking.

5 Place steak on grill with onions; cook steak 10 to 15 minutes, depending on thickness, for medium, or until desired doneness, turning steak once. Transfer steak to cutting board; let stand 10 minutes to allow juices to set for easier slicing. Transfer onions to bowl; cover and keep warm.

6 Wrap tortillas in foil; place tortillas near edge of grill over low heat until warm.

7 To serve, thinly slice steak. Place steak and onions on warm tortillas; top with some Guacamole and roll up to eat. Serve with lime wedges, sour cream, and remaining Guacamole.   *Makes 8 servings*

EACH SERVING: About 485 calories, 29 g protein, 52 g carbohydrate, 18 g total fat (5 g saturated), 7 g fiber, 49 mg cholesterol, 925 mg sodium

Guacamole (page 123)

3 tablespoons chili powder

1 teaspoon ground cumin

½ teaspoon salt

¼ teaspoon ground red pepper (cayenne)

1 beef skirt steak or flank steak (1¾ pounds)

2 large red onions (12 ounces each), sliced

1 tablespoon olive oil

8 (12-inch) low-fat flour tortillas

Lime wedges

Sour cream

Tex-Mex Burgers

For an all-out splurge, serve burgers with shredded lettuce, sliced red onion, extra salsa, and a topping of Guacamole (page 123). For a spicier burger, choose a medium to hot salsa and increase the chili powder to 2 teaspoons. Top the burger with sliced Monterey Jack, cover to melt the cheese, and you've got a Tex-Mex cheeseburger.

PREP: 5 MINUTES   GRILL: 12 MINUTES

1 pound lean ground beef (90%)
2 tablespoons minced onion
2 tablespoons bottled salsa
½ teaspoon salt
1 teaspoon chili powder
4 seeded rolls, split

1 Prepare grill.
2 In medium bowl, combine ground beef, onion, salsa, salt, and chili powder just until well blended but not overmixed. Shape mixture into 4 patties, each 1 inch thick, handling meat as little as possible. (Gentle handling is one of the keys to juicy burgers. Use a light hand when shaping patties, so the burgers won't come out compact and dry.)
3 Grill burgers over medium heat for 10 to 12 minutes for medium, or until desired doneness, turning once. Place rolls, cut side down, on grill over medium heat and toast, without turning, just until grill marks appear on cut side of rolls. Serve burgers on rolls.   *Makes 4 servings*

EACH SERVING: About 325 calories, 27 g protein, 23 g carbohydrate, 14 g total fat (5 g saturated), 1 g fiber, 70 mg cholesterol, 670 mg sodium

TIP
The best ground beef for burgers has some fat in it (about 10% works nicely) for juiciness and great flavor, so don't use the leanest ground beef.

Korean Steak

Definitely party food! Set out bowls of crisp romaine lettuce, rice, green onion, and sesame seeds and let each person assemble his or her own package. You may substitute either flank steak or a 1-inch-thick sirloin steak for the top round. Asian sesame oil gives rich flavor to the soy marinade.

PREP: 40 MINUTES PLUS MARINATING   GRILL: ABOUT 15 MINUTES

½ cup reduced-sodium soy sauce

2 tablespoons sugar

2 tablespoons minced peeled fresh ginger

2 tablespoons seasoned rice vinegar

1 tablespoon Asian sesame oil

¼ teaspoon ground red pepper (cayenne)

3 garlic cloves, crushed with garlic press

1 beef top round steak, 1 inch thick (about 1½ pounds)

1 cup regular long-grain rice

3 green onions, thinly sliced

1 tablespoon sesame seeds, toasted

1 head romaine lettuce, separated into leaves

1 In large zip-tight plastic bag, combine soy sauce, sugar, ginger, vinegar, sesame oil, ground red pepper, and garlic; add steak, turning to coat. Seal bag, pressing out excess air. Place on plate; refrigerate steak 1 to 4 hours to marinate, turning once.

2 Just before grilling steak, prepare rice as label directs; keep warm.

3 Prepare grill. Remove steak from bag; reserve marinade. Place steak on grill over medium heat and cook 14 to 15 minutes for medium-rare, or until desired doneness, turning steak once. Transfer to cutting board; let stand 10 minutes to allow juices to set for easier slicing.

4 In 1-quart saucepan, heat reserved marinade and ¼ cup water to boiling over high heat; boil 2 minutes.

5 To serve, thinly slice steak. Let each person place some steak slices, rice, green onions, and sesame seeds on a lettuce leaf, then drizzle with some cooked marinade. Fold sides of lettuce leaf over filling to make a package to eat like a sandwich.   *Makes 6 servings*

EACH SERVING: About 370 calories, 30 g protein, 35 g carbohydrate, 11 g total fat (3 g saturated), 2 g fiber, 69 mg cholesterol, 960 mg sodium

TIP
Toasting brings out the nutty flavor of sesame seeds. To toast, heat seeds in a small, dry skillet over moderate heat, stirring constantly, until fragrant and a shade darker.

Steaks with Chimichurri Sauce

This preparation works equally well with flank steak, skirt steak, or beef rib-eye. The sauce, a popular Argentinean blend, makes a toothsome topping for steaks and chicken alike. Serve with Grilled Polenta with Fontina (page 105) and a crisp green salad.

PREP: 20 MINUTES   GRILL: 15 TO 20 MINUTES

Chimichurri Sauce (page 123)

½ teaspoon chili powder

½ teaspoon sugar

½ teaspoon salt

¼ teaspoon ground cumin

2 boneless beef top loin steaks, each 1¼ inches thick (14 ounces each)

1 Prepare Chimichurri Sauce.

2 Prepare grill. In cup, mix chili powder, sugar, salt, and cumin. Rub steaks with chili mixture; set aside.

3 Place steaks on grill over medium heat. Cook 15 to 20 minutes for medium-rare, or until desired doneness, turning once. Let stand 10 minutes to allow juices to set for easier slicing.

4 Thinly slice steaks and serve with Chimichurri Sauce.

Makes 6 servings

EACH SERVING: About 375 calories, 25 g protein, 2 g carbohydrate, 29 g total fat (9 g saturated), 0 g fiber, 78 mg cholesterol, 335 mg sodium

TIP
Whip up an extra batch of the Chimichurri Sauce; you'll find it does wonders for a bowl of pasta, makes a great salad dressing, and stirred into a bit of mayonnaise, makes a wonderful sandwich spread.

Anise Beef Kabobs

We like to buy a sirloin steak and cut it into chunks to ensure equal-size pieces for even grilling. But, if you prefer, use precut beef cubes from your supermarket for the kabobs. The rub and meat can easily be doubled to feed a larger crowd. Serve with bowls of rice.

PREP: 10 MINUTES PLUS STANDING   GRILL: 8 TO 10 MINUTES

1 Soak wooden skewers in water 15 minutes.

2 Prepare grill. In mortar with pestle or in zip-tight plastic bag with rolling pin, crush anise seeds. In medium bowl, combine anise seeds, olive oil, salt, coarsely ground black pepper, and crushed red pepper, if using. Add steak chunks and toss to coat; let stand 10 minutes.

3 Thread steak chunks on skewers. Place skewers on grill over medium heat; cook 8 to 10 minutes for medium-rare, turning occasionally. *Makes 4 servings*

EACH SERVING: About 220 calories, 21 g protein, 0 g carbohydrate, 14 g total fat (5 g saturated), 0 g fiber, 68 mg cholesterol, 340 mg sodium

4 (8-inch) wooden skewers

1 teaspoon anise seeds or fennel seeds

2 teaspoons olive oil

½ teaspoon salt

¼ teaspoon coarsely ground black pepper

Pinch crushed red pepper (optional)

1 boneless beef top sirloin steak, 1 inch thick (1 pound) cut into 1¼-inch chunks

TIP
If you like, toss chunks of onion and peppers in a tablespoon of olive oil and thread on the skewers along with the meat.

Korean-Style Sesame Short Ribs

Marinating overnight makes these meaty ribs irresistible. Serve with a spicy cabbage slaw, a cool rice salad, and Glazed Japanese Eggplant (page 115). If you like, sprinkle the short ribs with sesame seeds and thinly sliced green onion just before serving.

PREP: 15 MINUTES PLUS OVERNIGHT TO MARINATE   GRILL: 20 TO 25 MINUTES

4   pounds beef chuck short ribs, cut into 2-inch pieces

½   cup reduced-sodium soy sauce

4   teaspoons minced peeled fresh ginger

2   teaspoons Asian sesame oil

3   large garlic cloves, minced

1 With sharp knife, slash meaty side of short ribs about ¼ inch deep diagonally at ½-inch intervals.

2 In zip-tight plastic bag, combine soy sauce, ginger, sesame oil, and garlic. Add short ribs, turning bag to coat. Seal bag, pressing out as much air as possible. Place bag in 13" by 9" pan and refrigerate overnight, turning once.

3 Prepare grill. Lift ribs from bag, reserving marinade. Place ribs on grill over medium heat; brush with reserved marinade and grill 20 to 25 minutes for medium-rare, turning ribs occasionally.

Makes 6 servings

EACH SERVING: About 745 calories, 34 g protein, 3 g carbohydrate, 65 g total fat (27 g saturated), 0 g fiber, 142 mg cholesterol, 880 mg sodium

TIP
Golden brown (roasted), nutty-tasting sesame oil is a flavoring oil as opposed to a cooking oil. Use a little to add flavor to stir-fries and Asian noodle dishes.

Mixed Grill with Asian Flavors

Serve up a big platter of shrimp, pork, beef, and chicken flavored 2 ways—half with an herb rub and half with a teriyaki-style marinade—so guests can customize their main courses.

PREP: 1 HOUR PLUS MARINATING GRILL: ABOUT 40 MINUTES

1 In 2 separate, jumbo zip-tight plastic bags, prepare Soy Marinade and Lime-Herb Rub. Add 1 flank steak, 1 pork tenderloin, and 5 chicken-breast halves to each bag, turning to coat. Seal bags, pressing out excess air. Refrigerate 30 minutes or up to 1 hour. Add 20 shrimp to each bag during last 10 minutes of marinating time.

2 Meanwhile, prepare Creamy Peanut Dipping Sauce.

3 Remove meat from bag with marinade; discard marinade. Remove meat from bag with rub. Place shrimp on skewers.

4 Place flank steaks and tenderloins on grill over medium heat. Cook flank steaks 15 to 20 minutes for medium-rare, or until desired doneness, turning once. Cook tenderloins 20 minutes, or until browned on the outside and slightly pink in the center, turning occasionally. Grill chicken-breast halves 10 to 12 minutes, turning once, until juices run clear when thickest part is pierced with tip of knife. Grill shrimp 4 to 6 minutes, until opaque throughout, turning once.

5 Thinly slice cooked meats; transfer to large platter. Cut chicken-breast halves lengthwise in half; transfer chicken and shrimp to platter. Serve with Creamy Peanut Dipping Sauce. *Makes 20 servings*

EACH SERVING: About 380 calories, 48 g protein, 10 g carbohydrate, 15 g total fat (4 g saturated), 0 g fiber, 131 mg cholesterol, 875 mg sodium

Soy Marinade (page 121)

Lime-Herb Rub (page 120)

2 beef flank steaks (1¼ pounds each)

2 whole pork tenderloins (1 pound each)

10 medium skinless, boneless chicken-breast halves (6 ounces each)

40 large shrimp, shelled and deveined

Creamy Peanut Dipping Sauce (page 124)

Stuffed Veal Chops

Thick, juicy veal chops, stuffed with a mixture of creamy cheese, roasted peppers, and basil, sit atop a bed of spicy greens. The combination of warm chop and cool greens is a real winner. Use a small paring knife to cut the pocket so that it is deep but not wide.

PREP: 15 MINUTES   GRILL: 10 TO 12 MINUTES

1 Prepare grill.

2 Prepare veal chops: Holding knife parallel to work surface, cut a horizontal pocket in each veal chop to form a deep pocket with as small an opening as possible.

3 In small bowl, mix roasted red peppers and 2 tablespoons chopped basil. Place Fontina cheese slices in veal pockets; spread red-pepper mixture over cheese. Sprinkle veal chops with ½ teaspoon salt and ½ teaspoon pepper.

4 Place chops on grill over medium-high heat and cook 10 to 12 minutes, until chops are lightly browned on both sides and just lose their pink color throughout, turning chops once.

5 Prepare arugula salad: In medium bowl, with wire whisk, mix olive oil, vinegar, remaining 1 tablespoon basil, mustard, remaining ⅛ teaspoon salt, and remaining ⅛ teaspoon pepper; add arugula, tossing to coat.

6 To serve, spoon arugula mixture onto platter; arrange chops on top.

Makes 4 servings

EACH SERVING: About 440 calories, 40 g protein, 2 g carbohydrate, 29 g total fat (11 g saturated), 1 g fiber, 181 mg cholesterol, 655 mg sodium

- 4 veal rib chops, each 1 inch thick (about 10 ounces each)
- ¼ cup roasted red peppers (one-third 7-ounce jar) drained and chopped
- 3 tablespoons chopped fresh basil leaves
- 2 ounces Fontina cheese, sliced
- ½ plus ⅛ teaspoon salt
- ½ plus ⅛ teaspoon coarsely ground black pepper
- 1 tablespoon olive oil
- 1 tablespoon balsamic vinegar
- ½ teaspoon Dijon mustard
- 4 ounces arugula, watercress, or baby spinach, tough stems removed

TIP
The grilled polenta on page 105 makes a delicious accompaniment to the chops. If you prefer a lower-fat dish, omit the cheese from the polenta.

Pork Tenderloins with Oregano

A 20-minute marination in lemon juice and herbs gives this lean cut of pork a zippy flavor. Twenty minutes is all it needs; the lemon juice will start to break down the meat fibers if it marinates much longer. To complete the dinner, serve with Grilled Vegetables Vinaigrette (page 107).

PREP: 10 MINUTES PLUS MARINATING   GRILL: ABOUT 20 MINUTES

¼ cup fresh lemon juice

2 tablespoons chopped fresh oregano leaves or 1 teaspoon dried oregano

2 tablespoons chopped fresh parsley leaves

2 pork tenderloins (about 12 ounces each)

1 tablespoon olive oil

½ teaspoon salt

¼ teaspoon coarsely ground black pepper

1 In large zip-tight plastic bag, combine lemon juice with 1 tablespoon each oregano and parsley. Add tenderloins, turning to coat. Seal bag, pressing out excess air. Place bag on plate; refrigerate tenderloins 20 minutes to marinate, turning once.

2 Prepare grill. Remove tenderloins from bag; discard marinade. In cup, mix olive oil, salt, pepper, and remaining 1 tablespoon each oregano and parsley; rub mixture all over tenderloins.

3 Place tenderloins on grill over medium heat and cook about 20 minutes, or until browned on the outside and still slightly pink in the center, turning occasionally (internal temperature of meat should be 160°F on meat thermometer). When tenderloins are done, transfer to warm large platter and let stand 5 minutes to set juices for easier slicing. Thinly slice tenderloins to serve.   *Makes 6 servings*

EACH SERVING: About 175 calories, 23 g protein, 1 g carbohydrate, 8 g total fat (3 g saturated), 1 g fiber, 71 mg cholesterol, 240 mg sodium

TIP
To prevent bacteria contamination from raw meat, always follow the "two-platter" rule: Use one platter for transporting meat, poultry, or fish to the grill, then use a second, clean one for the cooked food.

Spiced Pork Tenderloin with Mango Salsa

A simple blend of warm spices lends exotic flavor to lean and tender pork "cutlets." The salsa adds a tropical taste. Prepare the salsa several hours in advance, rub the pork with the spice mixture, and let it marinate while the grill heats up, then cook dinner in a matter of minutes.

PREP: 20 MINUTES   GRILL: 6 TO 7 MINUTES

1 Prepare Mango Salsa; cover and refrigerate.

2 Prepare grill. Cut each pork tenderloin lengthwise almost in half, being careful not to cut all the way through. Open and spread flat. Place each tenderloin between 2 sheets of plastic wrap; with meat mallet or rolling pin, pound to ¼-inch thickness. Cut each tenderloin into 4 pieces.

3 On waxed paper, mix flour, salt, cumin, coriander, cinnamon, and ginger; use to coat pork.

4 Place pork on grill over medium heat and cook 6 to 7 minutes, turning once, until lightly browned on both sides and pork just loses its pink color throughout. Serve with Mango Salsa.   *Makes 8 servings*

EACH SERVING: About 215 calories, 23 g protein, 15 g carbohydrate, 6 g total fat (2 g saturated), 1 g fiber, 71 mg cholesterol, 455 mg sodium

Mango Salsa (page 120)

2   pork tenderloins (about 1 pound each)

3   tablespoons all-purpose flour

1   teaspoon salt

1   teaspoon ground cumin

1   teaspoon ground coriander

½   teaspoon ground cinnamon

½   teaspoon ground ginger

TIP
Cut and pounded pork tenderloin is extremely versatile and can be used in most recipes that call for chicken cutlets.

Fennel-Orange Pork with Grilled Vegetables

Crushing the fennel seeds releases their flavor. The combination of fennel, thyme, and orange peel marries well with the richness of the pork. Radicchio and Belgian endive, with their slightly bitter taste, also serve as a counterbalance for the pork.

PREP: 15 MINUTES   GRILL: ABOUT 10 MINUTES

1   teaspoon fennel seeds

½   teaspoon dried thyme

¼   teaspoon coarsely ground black pepper

¾   teaspoon salt

1   teaspoon freshly grated orange peel

4   pork rib or loin chops, each 1 inch thick (about 6 ounces each)

1   tablespoon olive oil

1   tablespoon balsamic vinegar

2   heads radicchio di Treviso (about 4 ounces each), each cut lengthwise in half, or 1 large round head radicchio (about 8 ounces), cut into 8 wedges

2   large heads Belgian endive (about 5 ounces each), each cut lengthwise into quarters

Orange wedges and lemon leaves for garnish (optional)

1 Prepare grill. In mortar with pestle or in zip-tight plastic bag with rolling pin, crush fennel seeds with thyme, pepper, and ½ teaspoon salt. Stir orange peel into fennel-seed mixture.

2 With hand, rub both sides of pork chops with fennel-seed mixture.

3 In medium bowl, mix olive oil, balsamic vinegar, and remaining ¼ teaspoon salt. Add radicchio and endive to bowl and gently toss to coat.

4 Place pork chops on grill over medium heat. Cook chops 5 minutes. Turn chops and add vegetables to grill. Cook pork chops and vegetables about 5 minutes longer, or until chops have just a hint of pink color in center and vegetables are browned. Serve pork chops with grilled vegetables. Garnish with orange wedges and lemon leaves if you like.   *Makes 4 servings*

EACH SERVING: About 250 calories, 23 g protein, 5 g carbohydrate, 15 g total fat (4 g saturated), 2 g fiber, 61 mg cholesterol, 490 mg sodium

> TIP
> If you can't find radicchio, a burgundy-colored, slightly bitter Italian chicory, substitute 2 more heads of Belgian endive.

Meat   70

Ribs Supreme

Only 15 minutes of grilling time! The trick: Steam the seasoned ribs for an hour in the oven up to 2 days before barbecuing. With both the ribs and the BBQ sauce prepared in advance, this could easily become a part of your summer weeknight repertoire.

PREP: 1 HOUR 15 MINUTES GRILL: 15 MINUTES

1 Preheat oven to 350°F. In cup, mix ginger, lemon peel, salt, and garlic until combined. Rub ginger mixture all over ribs.

2 Place ribs in large roasting pan (15½" by 11½"), overlapping slightly. Pour 2 cups boiling water into roasting pan. Cover pan tightly with foil. Steam ribs 1 hour.

3 Meanwhile, prepare Secret-Recipe BBQ Sauce.

4 Carefully remove foil from roasting pan (escaping steam is very hot). Remove ribs from roasting pan; discard water. Ribs may be grilled immediately, or refrigerated up to 2 days before grilling.

5 Prepare grill. Place ribs, meat side up, on grill over medium heat; cook 5 minutes, turning once. Turn ribs over; brush with some BBQ sauce and grill 5 minutes. Turn ribs over again, brush with more BBQ sauce, and grill 5 minutes longer. Cut racks into 2-rib portions; serve with remaining sauce. *Makes 6 servings*

EACH SERVING: About 615 calories, 36 g protein, 16 g carbohydrate, 44 g total fat (16 g saturated), 1 g fiber, 172 mg cholesterol, 760 mg sodium

- 4 teaspoons grated peeled fresh ginger
- 2 teaspoons grated fresh lemon peel
- ¾ teaspoon salt
- 2 garlic cloves, crushed with garlic press
- 4 racks pork baby back ribs (about 1 pound each)
- 2 cups Secret-Recipe BBQ Sauce (page 122)

TIP
When buying baby backs, look for ribs that are meaty with a minimum of visible fat.

Plum-Good Baby Back Ribs

Licorice-flavored star anise—one of the spices in Chinese five-spice powder—gives these
ribs their distinctive appeal. The ribs can be cooked in the seasoned liquid up to 2 days ahead, cooled, covered,
and refrigerated. Remove the ribs from the refrigerator while the grill heats, then proceed with the recipe.

PREP: 1 HOUR   GRILL: 15 TO 20 MINUTES

4   racks pork baby back ribs (about 1 pound each)

12   whole black peppercorns

2   bay leaves

10   whole star anise

2   cinnamon sticks (each 3 inches long)

¼   cup soy sauce

1   jar (12 ounces) plum jam (1 cup)

1   tablespoon grated peeled fresh ginger

1   garlic clove, crushed with garlic press

1 In 8-quart saucepot, heat ribs, peppercorns, bay leaves, 4 star anise, 1 cinnamon stick, and enough water to cover, to boiling over high heat. Reduce heat to low; cover and simmer 50 minutes to 1 hour, until ribs are fork-tender. Remove ribs to platter. If not serving right away, cover and refrigerate until ready to serve.

2 Prepare glaze: In 1-quart saucepan, heat soy sauce, remaining 6 star anise and 1 cinnamon stick to boiling over high heat. Reduce heat to low; cover and simmer 5 minutes. Remove from heat; let stand, covered, 5 minutes. Strain mixture into bowl; discard star anise and cinnamon. Stir in plum jam, grated ginger, and garlic.

3 Prepare grill. Place ribs on grill over medium heat. Cook 10 minutes, turning once, until browned. Brush ribs with some glaze and cook 5 to 10 minutes, brushing with remaining glaze and turning frequently.

Makes 6 servings

EACH SERVING: About 690 calories, 37 g protein, 38 g carbohydrate, 43 g total fat (16 g saturated), 1 g fiber, 172 mg cholesterol, 860 mg sodium

TIP
Star anise, a star-shaped, licorice-flavored spice, can be found on the spice shelf or gourmet section of your supermarket.

Southern Peach Pork Chops

Juicy July peaches hot off the grill are perfect with tender, seared meat. If you'd like more of a kick from the curry rub, try using Madras curry powder; it is somewhat hotter than regular curry powder. Lightly brush the grill with oil before heating to prevent the jam from sticking.

PREP: 15 MINUTES   GRILL: ABOUT 15 MINUTES

1 Prepare grill. In cup, stir curry powder, brown sugar, olive oil, salt, cinnamon, pepper, and garlic.

2 With hands, rub both sides of pork chops with curry mixture.

3 Brush cut side of peach halves and 1 side of chops with some jam. Place peaches, jam side down, and chops, jam side up, on grill over medium heat; cook 5 minutes.

4 Turn chops and peaches over and brush grilled side of chops with some jam; cook 5 minutes longer. Remove peaches from grill when browned; place on platter. Turn chops and brush with remaining jam; cook 2 to 3 minutes longer, until chops are browned on the outside and still slightly pink on the inside. Place chops on platter with peaches; garnish with arugula.   *Makes 4 servings*

EACH SERVING: About 500 calories, 21 g protein, 49 g carbohydrate, 26 g total fat (9 g saturated), 4 g fiber, 77 mg cholesterol, 360 mg sodium

1 tablespoon curry powder

1 tablespoon brown sugar

1 tablespoon olive oil

½ teaspoon salt

¼ teaspoon ground cinnamon

Pinch coarsely ground black pepper

1 garlic clove, crushed with garlic press

4 pork loin chops, each ¾ inch thick (about 5 ounces each)

4 large peaches, each cut in half and pitted

½ cup peach or apricot jam or preserves

Arugula for garnish

TIP
Peach halves, brushed with jam and grilled, make a wonderful summer dessert.

75   Meat

Charbroiled Pork Chops with Corn Salsa

Nothing says summer better than grilled meat and sweet corn. After a 15-minute marinade, meaty chops are flame-cooked, then topped with a quick garden salsa. Jalapeños vary in their degree of heat, so taste a small piece before you use it. If you'd like your salsa hotter, add more ground red pepper.

PREP: 15 MINUTES PLUS MARINATING   GRILL: 10 TO 12 MINUTES

2 tablespoons vegetable oil

2 tablespoons fresh lime juice

½ teaspoon salt

¼ teaspoon ground red pepper (cayenne)

4 bone-in pork loin or rib chops, each ¾ inch thick (about 6 ounces each)

2 cups corn kernels cut from cobs (3 to 4 ears)

2 medium ripe tomatoes, chopped

1 small red onion, finely chopped

1 jalapeño chile, seeded and minced

Cilantro sprigs for garnish

1 In medium bowl, with wire whisk or fork, mix oil, lime juice, salt, and ground red pepper. Spoon half of oil mixture into pie plate. Add pork chops to mixture in pie plate; turn to coat. Marinate pork 15 minutes at room temperature or 30 minutes in the refrigerator, turning chops occasionally.

2 Prepare grill. Meanwhile, into oil mixture in bowl, stir corn kernels, tomato, red onion, and jalapeño. Let salsa stand at room temperature until ready to serve.

3 Place pork chops on grill over medium heat; discard marinade in pie plate. Cook chops 10 to 12 minutes, until browned on the outside and still slightly pink on the inside, turning once. Serve pork chops with corn salsa. Garnish with cilantro. *Makes 4 servings*

EACH SERVING: About 420 calories, 23 g protein, 22 g carbohydrate, 28 g total fat (9 g saturated), 4 g fiber, 78 mg cholesterol, 240 mg sodium

TIP
This corn salsa would also be delicious served alongside grilled steaks, chicken, or shrimp.

Meat 76

Pork Steaks with Plum Glaze

Our 1973 edition of *The Good Housekeeping Cookbook* explained how to cut a pork tenderloin into 4 lean and juicy steaks—a family secret from Zoe Coulson, GH food editor from 1968 to 1975. We used the same technique here: Slice tenderloin lengthwise almost in half, pound, then cut into serving-size pieces. Thanks, Zoe!

PREP: 10 MINUTES   GRILL: ABOUT 6 MINUTES

1 Prepare grill. Cut pork tenderloin lengthwise, almost in half, being careful not to cut all the way through. Open and spread flat. Place tenderloin between 2 sheets of plastic wrap; with meat mallet or rolling pin, pound to about ¼-inch thickness. Cut the tenderloin into 4 pieces; sprinkle with salt and pepper.

2 In small bowl, mix plum jam, brown sugar, ginger, lemon juice, cinnamon, and garlic. Brush 1 side of each pork steak and cut side of each plum half with plum-jam glaze. Place pork and plums on grill, glaze side down, over medium heat and cook 3 minutes. Brush steaks and plums with remaining glaze; turn and cook 3 minutes longer, or until steaks are lightly browned on both sides and just lose their pink color throughout and plums are hot.   *Makes 4 servings*

EACH SERVING: About 325 calories, 24 g protein, 44 g carbohydrate, 7 g total fat (2 g saturated), 3 g fiber, 71 mg cholesterol, 65 mg sodium

1 pork tenderloin (about 1 pound)

1   teaspoon salt

¼ teaspoon coarsely ground black pepper

½ cup plum jam or preserves

1 tablespoon brown sugar

1 tablespoon grated peeled fresh ginger

1 tablespoon fresh lemon juice

½ teaspoon ground cinnamon

2 garlic cloves, crushed with garlic press

4 large plums (about 1 pound), each cut in half and pitted

TIP
Perfect plums are firm, but give slightly when pressed. Look for good color but don?t worry about a gray filmy coating, which is typical of many varieties of plums.

Teriyaki Pork Chops

We love this teriyaki sauce made with soy sauce, fresh ginger, and brown sugar. This soy marinade is perfect for chicken thighs as well as pork. The pineapple is a welcome accompaniment to the pork and can also be grilled on its own and served for dessert.

PREP: 15 MINUTES PLUS MARINATING   GRILL: 15 TO 20 MINUTES

2 green onions, sliced

⅓ cup reduced-sodium soy sauce

2 tablespoons grated peeled fresh ginger

2 tablespoons plus ¼ cup packed light brown sugar

4 pork loin chops, each ¾ inch thick (about 8 ounces each)

1 small pineapple

   Green-onion strips for garnish

1 In 13" by 9" glass baking dish, prepare teriyaki sauce: With fork, mix sliced green onions, soy sauce, ginger, and 2 tablespoons brown sugar. Add pork chops, turning to coat with teriyaki mixture. Let stand 20 minutes to marinate.

2 Prepare grill. Meanwhile, cut off rind from pineapple, then cut pineapple crosswise into ½-inch-thick slices. Rub pineapple slices with remaining ¼ cup brown sugar.

3 Place pineapple slices on grill over medium heat. Cook pineapple slices 15 to 20 minutes, until browned on both sides, turning slices occasionally. After pineapple has cooked 10 minutes, add pork chops and cook until lightly browned on both sides and chops just lose their pink color throughout, about 10 minutes. Turn chops occasionally and brush with remaining teriyaki mixture halfway through cooking time. Serve pork chops with grilled pineapple slices. Garnish with green-onion strips. *Makes 4 servings*

EACH SERVING: About 645 calories, 33 g protein, 48 g carbohydrate, 37 g total fat (13 g saturated), 3 g fiber, 124 mg cholesterol, 1,040 mg sodium

TIP
To prepare a fresh pineapple, use a sharp knife and cut off the leaves at the base, then slice off the bottom rind. Stand fruit upright and slice the rind from the sides in downward strokes. Remove any "eyes" that are left with the tip of a sharp knife.

Meat 80

Sausage & Pepper Grill

Grill Italian hard rolls and serve the sausage and peppers on top for a hearty open-faced sandwich reminiscent of those found at street fairs. If you'd prefer, toss the grilled sausages and vegetables with a bowl of cooked ziti, add some grated Parmesan cheese, and serve.

PREP: 15 MINUTES   GRILL: 15 TO 20 MINUTES

1 In cup, mix balsamic vinegar, brown sugar, salt, and black pepper. In large bowl, toss red and green peppers and onions with olive oil to coat.

2 Prepare grill. Place sausages and vegetables on grill over medium heat. Cook sausages 15 to 20 minutes, turning occasionally, until golden brown and cooked through. Cook vegetables about 15 minutes or until tender, turning occasionally, and brushing with some balsamic mixture during last 3 minutes of cooking. Transfer vegetables and sausages to platter as they finish cooking.

3 To serve, cut sausages into 2-inch diagonal slices. Drizzle remaining balsamic mixture over vegetables.   *Makes 4 servings*

EACH SERVING: About 500 calories, 27 g protein, 19 g carbohydrate, 36 g total fat (12 g saturated), 3 g fiber, 97 mg cholesterol, 1,450 mg sodium

⅓   cup balsamic vinegar

1   teaspoon brown sugar

½   teaspoon salt

¼   teaspoon coarsely ground black pepper

2   medium red peppers, cut into 1½-inch-wide strips

2   medium green peppers, cut into 1½-inch-wide strips

2   large red onions (about 8 ounces each), each cut into 6 wedges

1   tablespoon olive oil

¾   pound sweet Italian sausage links

¾   pound hot Italian sausage links

TIP
Adding a small amount of brown sugar to ordinary balsamic vinegar gives it a smooth, mellow flavor similar to an aged vinegar. Try this trick the next time you make a balsamic vinegar dressing.

81   Meat

Spiced Butterflied Lamb

For a cool and tangy sauce, a jar of mango chutney, available at the supermarket, can be chopped and added to yogurt and served with the lamb. A crisp green or cucumber salad tossed with chopped fresh cilantro and basmati rice would be welcome additions to this Indian-style lamb.

PREP: 10 MINUTES PLUS MARINATING   GRILL: 20 TO 35 MINUTES

1   cup plain low-fat yogurt

8   garlic cloves, peeled

1   piece fresh ginger (about 2 inches), peeled and coarsely chopped

1   tablespoon ground coriander

1   tablespoon ground cumin

2   tablespoons fresh lemon juice

2   teaspoons salt

¼   to ½ teaspoon ground red pepper (cayenne)

3   pounds boneless butterflied leg of lamb*

*Ask butcher to bone a 4-pound lamb leg shank half and slit the meat lengthwise to spread open like a book.

1 In blender, combine yogurt, garlic, ginger, coriander, cumin, lemon juice, salt, and ground red pepper, and blend until smooth. Pour yogurt mixture into large zip-tight plastic bag; add lamb, turning to coat. Seal bag, pressing out excess air. Place bag on plate; refrigerate lamb 1 hour, turning occasionally. (Do not marinate more than 2 hours or texture of meat will change.)

2 Remove lamb from bag. Pour marinade into small bowl and reserve.

3 Prepare grill. Place lamb on grill over medium heat; cook 15 minutes, turning once. Brush both sides of lamb with reserved marinade and cook 10 to 20 minutes longer for medium-rare, or until desired doneness, turning lamb occasionally. Thickness of butterflied lamb will vary throughout; cut off sections of lamb as they are cooked and place on cutting board.   *Makes 10 servings*

EACH SERVING: About 280 calories, 27 g protein, 3 g carbohydrate, 17 g total fat (7 g saturated), 0 g fiber, 95 mg cholesterol, 550 mg sodium

> **TIP**
> For seedless juice, place a lemon half cut side down on a square of cheesecloth. Bring cheesecloth up over the top and tie with a twist-tie, then squeeze out the juice, seed-free.

Aromatic Leg of Lamb

We love this mixture of crushed fennel, cumin, and coriander seeds on lamb chops and chicken cutlets as well as leg of lamb. If you don't have a mortar and pestle and find crushing seeds with a rolling pin tedious, consider purchasing a small grinder intended for coffee beans; keep it just for spices, then buy whole seeds and grind them yourself.

PREP: 20 MINUTES   GRILL: 15 TO 25 MINUTES

3   pounds boneless butterflied leg of lamb*

3   garlic cloves, each cut in half and crushed with side of chef's knife

2   teaspoons fennel seeds

2   teaspoons cumin seeds

2   teaspoons coriander seeds

1   tablespoon olive oil

1½ teaspoons salt

    Lemon wedges (optional)

*Ask butcher to bone a 4-pound lamb leg shank half and slit the meat lengthwise to spread open like a book.

1 Rub lamb with cut side of garlic cloves; discard garlic. In mortar with pestle, crush fennel, cumin, and coriander seeds. (Or, place seeds in heavy-weight zip-tight plastic bag; use rolling pin to crush seeds.)

2 In small bowl, combine crushed seeds with olive oil and salt. With hand, rub lamb with crushed-seed mixture.

3 Place lamb on grill over medium heat. Cook 15 to 25 minutes for medium-rare, or until desired doneness, turning lamb occasionally. Thickness of butterflied lamb will vary throughout; cut off sections of lamb as they are cooked and place on cutting board.

4 Serve lamb with lemon wedges if you like.   *Makes 10 servings*

EACH SERVING: About 280 calories, 26 g protein, 1 g carbohydrate, 18 g total fat (7 g saturated), 0 g fiber, 94 mg cholesterol, 415 mg sodium

> ### TIP
> Rub lamb with spice mixture, cover, and refrigerate as long as overnight. Bring to room temperature before grilling.

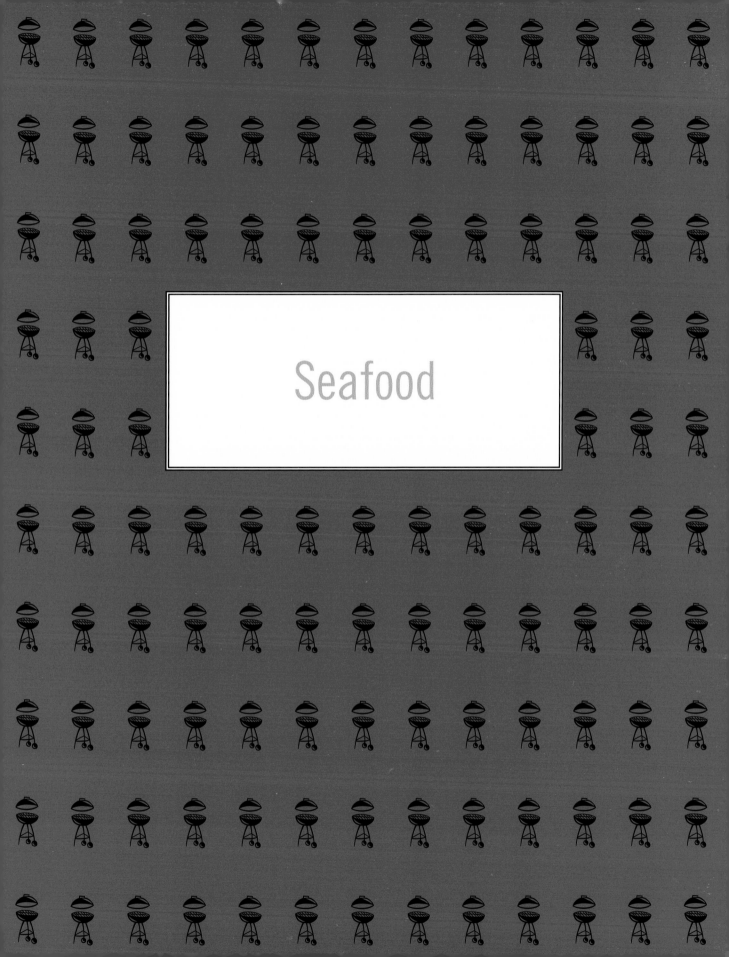

Seafood

Salmon with Dill & Caper Sauce

Anchovy paste is available in tubes in the dairy section of many supermarkets. If you can't find anchovy paste, substitute 2 anchovy fillets. Mash the fillets with the flat side of a knife until they're the consistency of a smooth paste. Serve the salmon with Cucumber Relish (page 122), if you'd like.

PREP: 10 MINUTES   GRILL: 10 MINUTES

¼ cup drained capers, chopped

2 tablespoons fresh dill, chopped

2 tablespoons fresh lemon juice

2 teaspoons sugar

2 teaspoons anchovy paste

1 salmon fillet (2 pounds), skin on

¼ teaspoon salt

Fresh dill

Lemon wedges

1 In small bowl, mix capers, dill, lemon juice, sugar, and anchovy paste.

2 With tweezers, remove any small bones from salmon fillet; sprinkle with salt.

3 Place salmon in lightly greased fish basket; brush all caper sauce on flesh side only. Place fish basket on rack on grill. Over medium heat, cook salmon 5 minutes on each side, or until salmon flakes easily when tested with a fork. Garnish with fresh dill and lemon wedges.

Makes 8 servings

EACH SERVING: About 210 calories, 22 g protein, 2 g carbohydrate, 12 g total fat (2 g saturated), 0 g fiber, 64 mg cholesterol, 395 mg sodium

TIP

Stir together chopped dill or tarragon, fresh lemon juice, a fruity olive oil, salt, and pepper and serve as a sauce to spoon over any grilled fish.

Honey-Lime Salmon

Rich salmon fillets stand up to an assertively spiced rub. Marinate the salmon up to 8 hours before grilling.
On the side, serve coleslaw dressed with a vinaigrette or a salad of thick-sliced summer tomatoes
and crunchy cucumbers.

PREP: 10 MINUTES   GRILL: ABOUT 10 MINUTES

3 tablespoons honey

1 teaspoon ground cumin

1 teaspoon ground coriander

¾ teaspoon salt

¾ teaspoon grated fresh lime peel

¼ teaspoon coarsely ground black pepper

4 pieces salmon fillet, each ¾ inch thick (about 6 ounces each), skin removed

3 tablespoons chopped fresh cilantro leaves

Lime wedges

1 In cup, mix honey, cumin, coriander, salt, lime peel, pepper, and 1 teaspoon very hot water until blended.

2 With tweezers, remove any bones from salmon. With hands, rub honey-spice mixture all over salmon pieces.

3 Lightly oil grill. Place salmon on grill over medium heat and cook 4 minutes. With wide metal spatula, carefully turn salmon over; cook 4 to 5 minutes longer, just until salmon turns opaque throughout and flakes easily when tested with a fork.

4 Sprinkle salmon with cilantro and serve with lime wedges.

Makes 4 servings

EACH SERVING: About 350 calories, 32 g protein, 14 g carbohydrate, 18 g total fat (4 g saturated), 0 g fiber, 95 mg cholesterol, 535 mg sodium

> TIP
> You can substitute red snapper or bluefish fillets for the salmon.

Sicilian-Style Swordfish with Pasta

Chunks of grilled fish are tossed with pasta in a light vinaigrette made with fresh mint and tomato. If you can't find fresh mint, substitute fresh basil or parsley.

PREP: 15 MINUTES PLUS MARINATING   GRILL: 8 TO 10 MINUTES

1 In large bowl, combine tomatoes, mint, vinegar, garlic, 2 tablespoons olive oil, ½ teaspoon salt, and ¼ teaspoon pepper. Cover and let stand 30 minutes.

2 In cup, combine orange peel, remaining 1 tablespoon olive oil, ¼ teaspoon salt, and remaining ¼ teaspoon pepper; brush on both sides of swordfish.

3 Place swordfish on grill over medium heat; cook 8 to 10 minutes, or until just opaque throughout, turning once. Transfer swordfish to cutting board and cut into 1-inch pieces.

4 Meanwhile, prepare pasta in boiling salted water as package directs. Drain.

5 Add swordfish and pasta to tomato mixture; toss.   *Makes 6 servings*

EACH SERVING: About 440 calories, 24 g protein, 61 g carbohydrate, 11 g total fat (2 g saturated), 3 g fiber, 26 mg cholesterol, 430 mg sodium

3   ripe medium tomatoes, cut into ½-inch chunks (about 2½ cups)

¼   cup chopped fresh mint

1   tablespoon red wine vinegar

1   small garlic clove, minced

3   tablespoons olive oil

    Salt

½   teaspoon coarsely ground black pepper

1   teaspoon grated orange peel

1   swordfish steak, 1 inch thick (about 1 pound)

1   pound penne or bow-tie pasta

TIP
For an added Sicilian touch, toast pine nuts and add to the pasta along with a handful of golden raisins.

Jamaican Jerk Catfish with Grilled Pineapple

Other fish fillets like sole, flounder, snapper, and bluefish work well with these zesty flavors, too. A very versatile seasoning, jerk also does wonders for grilled chicken and pork. Add another jalapeño or some crushed red peppers if you'd like a spicier jerk.

PREP: 15 MINUTES   GRILL: 10 TO 12 MINUTES

1 In medium bowl, mix green onions, jalapeño, vinegar, Worcestershire, ginger, vegetable oil, thyme, allspice, and salt until combined. Add catfish fillets to bowl, turning to coat; let stand 5 minutes.

2 Meanwhile, rub pineapple wedges or slices with brown sugar.

3 Place pineapple and catfish fillets on grill. Spoon half of jerk mixture remaining in bowl on catfish. Cook pineapple and catfish 5 minutes. Turn over pineapple and catfish. Spoon remaining jerk mixture on fish and cook 5 to 7 minutes longer, until fish flakes easily when tested with a fork, and pineapple is golden brown. *Makes 4 servings*

EACH SERVING: About 350 calories, 23 g protein, 35 g carbohydrate, 14 g total fat (3 g saturated), 3 g fiber, 47 mg cholesterol, 280 mg sodium

- 2 green onions, chopped
- 1 jalapeño chile, seeded and chopped
- 2 tablespoons white wine vinegar
- 2 tablespoons Worcestershire sauce
- 1 tablespoon minced peeled fresh ginger
- 1 tablespoon vegetable oil
- 1¼ teaspoons dried thyme
- 1 teaspoon ground allspice
- ¼ teaspoon salt
- 4 catfish fillets (about 5 ounces each)
- 1 small pineapple, cut lengthwise into 4 wedges or crosswise into ½-inch-thick slices
- 2 tablespoons brown sugar

TIP
Fresh jalapeño peppers vary in their degree of heat, while pickled jalapeños from a jar are always hot. Feel free to substitute jarred for fresh in most recipes.

Shrimp Sonoma

Some of the sweetest dried tomatoes we've tried come from the Sonoma Valley in California. Choose dried tomatoes that are plump, rather than dry and leathery. Make a batch of Veggie Kabobs (page 110) and grill them alongside the shrimp. Serve on a bed of couscous seasoned with extra virgin olive oil.

PREP: 25 MINUTES PLUS STANDING   GRILL: 8 TO 10 MINUTES

1   ounce dried tomatoes without salt
1   cup boiling water
1½ pounds large shrimp
2   tablespoons fresh lemon juice
2   tablespoons olive oil
½   teaspoon salt
½   teaspoon crushed red pepper

1 Place dried tomatoes in small bowl. Pour boiling water over tomatoes; let stand while preparing shrimp.

2 Meanwhile, pull off legs from shrimp. Insert tip of kitchen shears under shell of each shrimp and snip along back to tail, cutting about ¼ inch deep to expose dark vein. Leaving shell on, rinse shrimp to remove vein. Place shrimp in bowl.

3 Prepare grill. Drain dried tomatoes, reserving ¼ cup soaking liquid.

4 In blender or in food processor with knife blade attached, blend tomatoes with reserved soaking liquid, lemon juice, olive oil, salt, and pepper until well blended. Pour over shrimp.

5 On 4 long skewers, thread shrimp. Place skewers on grill over medium heat; grill 8 to 10 minutes, until shrimp turn opaque throughout, turning skewers occasionally, and basting with any remaining tomato mixture.   *Makes 6 servings*

EACH SERVING: About 140 calories, 20 g protein, 3 g carbohydrate, 5 g total fat (1 g saturated), 1 g fiber, 140 mg cholesterol, 290 mg sodium

TIP
When shopping for shrimp, look for firm, shiny shells without black spots.

Asian Tuna Burgers

Finely chop fish by hand for a light texture; using a food processor will make the patties dense and dry. Serve with pickled ginger, with or without a bun. Cucumber Relish (page 122) would be the perfect condiment to serve with these tasty burgers.

PREP: 15 MINUTES   GRILL: 6 TO 7 MINUTES

1   tuna steak (about 1 pound)

1   green onion, thinly sliced

2   tablespoons reduced-sodium soy sauce

1   teaspoon grated peeled fresh ginger

¼   teaspoon coarsely ground black pepper

¼   cup plain dried bread crumbs

2   tablespoons sesame seeds

    Nonstick cooking spray

1 Prepare grill. With large chef's knife, finely chop tuna. Place tuna in medium bowl and mix in green onion, soy sauce, ginger, and pepper until combined.

2 Shape tuna mixture into four 3-inch round patties (mixture will be very soft and moist).

3 On waxed paper, combine bread crumbs and sesame seeds. With hands, carefully press patties, one at a time, into bread-crumb mixture, turning to coat both sides. Spray both sides of tuna patties with nonstick spray.

4 Place tuna patties on grill over medium heat and cook 6 to 7 minutes, until browned on the outside and still slightly pink in the center for medium-rare, or until desired doneness, turning patties once.   *Makes 4 servings*

EACH SERVING: About 210 calories, 26 g protein, 7 g carbohydrate, 8 g total fat (2 g saturated), 1 g fiber, 38 mg cholesterol, 400 mg sodium

TIP
If you can't imagine a burger of any sort without ketchup, try a combination of hoisin (Chinese plum sauce) and ketchup as a topping.

Thai Snapper

Tender fillets are seasoned with lime and ginger and cooked in a foil packet. Don't be tempted to assemble the packets too soon before grilling; the lime juice will start to "cook" the fillets, giving them a mushy texture. Instead, cut the vegetables and mix the lime juice mixture several hours ahead and assemble the packets just before cooking.

PREP: 30 MINUTES   GRILL: 8 MINUTES

1 In small bowl, mix lime juice, fish sauce, olive oil, ginger, sugar, and garlic.

2 From roll of foil, cut four 16" by 12" sheets. Fold each sheet crosswise in half and open up again.

3 Place 1 red snapper fillet, skin side down, on half of each piece of foil. Top with carrot, green onion, then cilantro leaves. Spoon the lime-juice mixture over the snapper and vegetables. Fold other half of foil over fish. Fold and crimp foil edges all around to create 4 sealed packets.

4 Place packets on grill over medium heat; cook 8 minutes.

5 To serve: With kitchen shears, cut an X in the top of each packet so steam can escape. (When packets are open, check that fish flakes when tested with a fork.) *Makes 4 servings*

EACH SERVING: About 230 calories, 36 g protein, 5 g carbohydrate, 6 g total fat (1 g saturated), 1 g fiber, 63 mg cholesterol, 270 mg sodium

3 tablespoons fresh lime juice

1 tablespoon Asian fish sauce*

1 tablespoon olive oil

1 teaspoon grated peeled fresh ginger

½ teaspoon sugar

½ teaspoon minced garlic

4 red snapper fillets (6 ounces each)

1 large carrot, cut into 2¼-inch-long matchstick-thin strips

1 large green onion, thinly sliced

¼ cup packed fresh cilantro leaves

Asian fish sauce (nuoc nam) is a thin, translucent, salty, brown liquid extracted from salted, fermented fish. This condiment is used mostly in Thai and Vietnamese cooking. It can be purchased in the Asian sections of some grocery stores.

TIP

Serve the snapper with Thai coconut rice. To make, bring 1 cup salted water and 1 cup unsweetened canned coconut milk to a boil in a large saucepan. Add 1 cup rinsed jasmine rice. Reduce heat to low and cook, covered, until rice is tender, about 20 minutes.

Spiced Salmon Steaks

Juicy summer-ripe red and yellow tomatoes are a cool and easy go-along for this entrée. Dress the tomatoes with a fruity olive oil and a sprinkling of finely shredded basil. Try this preparation with thick bluefish fillets; the spice mixture is a delicious complement to the richness of the fish.

PREP: 10 MINUTES   GRILL: 8 MINUTES

1 Prepare grill. In cup, mix chili powder, brown sugar, cumin, thyme, salt, and olive oil.

2 With tweezers, remove any small bones from salmon steaks.

3 With hands, rub spice mixture over both sides of salmon steaks. Place salmon on grill over medium heat. Cook about 8 minutes, or until salmon flakes easily when tested with a fork, turning once. Serve with lemon wedges if you like.   *Makes 4 servings*

EACH SERVING: About 405 calories, 40 g protein, 4 g carbohydrate, 24 g total fat (5 g saturated), 1 g fiber, 118 mg cholesterol, 720 mg sodium

1 tablespoon chili powder

2 teaspoons light brown sugar

1 teaspoon ground cumin

1 teaspoon dried thyme

1 teaspoon salt

2 teaspoons olive oil

4 salmon steaks, each ¾ inch thick (about 8 ounces each)

Lemon wedges (optional)

TIP
This recipe doubles easily. Prepare a double batch, serve half, and refrigerate the remainder. Serve the salmon chilled or at room temperature the next day.

Shrimp & Scallop Kabobs

Shrimp and scallops cook in a flash and require no marinating. If the scallops are very large, halve them horizontally. Don't substitute bay scallops; they're small and would cook too quickly. If you like, serve with Pineapple Salsa (page 123) and a bowl of rice.

PREP: 20 MINUTES   GRILL: 6 TO 8 MINUTES

1   pound large shrimp

1   pound large sea scallops

3   tablespoons soy sauce

3   tablespoons seasoned rice vinegar

2   tablespoons grated peeled fresh ginger

1   tablespoon brown sugar

1   tablespoon Asian sesame oil

2   garlic cloves, crushed with garlic press

1   bunch green onions, cut diagonally into 3-inch-long pieces

12   cherry tomatoes

1 Prepare grill. Shell and devein shrimp, leaving tail part of shell on if you like; rinse with cold running water. Rinse scallops well to remove sand from crevices. Pat shrimp and scallops dry with paper towels.

2 In large bowl, mix soy sauce, rice vinegar, ginger, brown sugar, sesame oil, and garlic; add shrimp and scallops, tossing to coat.

3 Onto 6 long metal skewers, alternately thread shrimp, scallops, green onions, and cherry tomatoes. Place skewers on grill over medium heat; cook 6 to 8 minutes, until shrimp and scallops are opaque throughout, turning skewers occasionally, and basting shrimp and scallops with any remaining soy mixture halfway through cooking.

Makes 6 servings

EACH SERVING: About 185 calories, 26 g protein, 10 g carbohydrate, 4 g total fat (1 g saturated), 1 g fiber, 118 mg cholesterol, 880 mg sodium

TIP
The soy mixture can be made several hours in advance, covered, and refrigerated. Whisk to combine before adding the shrimp and scallops.

Grilled Halibut with Fresh Dill

If fresh halibut is not available, substitute swordfish or tuna steaks. White-wine Worcestershire sauce is somewhat more delicate in flavor than the original Worcestershire and is particularly good with seafood and poultry. If you can't find white-wine Worcestershire, use 3 tablespoons of original Worcestershire and add 1 tablespoon of water.

PREP: 5 MINUTES PLUS MARINATING   GRILL: 10 MINUTES

¼ cup white-wine Worcestershire sauce

2 tablespoons fresh lemon juice

1 tablespoon olive oil

1 tablespoon minced fresh dill

¼ teaspoon coarsely ground black pepper

2 halibut steaks, each 1 inch thick (about 12 ounces each)

1 In medium bowl, stir Worcestershire, lemon juice, olive oil, dill, and pepper. Place halibut in large zip-tight plastic bag. Add Worcestershire mixture. Seal bag, pressing out excess air. Place bag on plate; refrigerate at least 2 hours, turning bag over once.

2 Prepare grill. Place halibut on grill over low heat, reserving marinade. Cook, turning occasionally, and basting frequently with reserved marinade, 10 minutes, or until opaque throughout.

Makes 4 servings

EACH SERVING: About 195 calories, 29 g protein, 3 g carbohydrate, 7 g total fat (1 g saturated), 0 g fiber, 45 mg cholesterol, 200 mg sodium

TIP
Stir up an extra batch of the Worcestershire mixture and serve as a sauce for the fish.

Seafood **100**

Vegetables
& Side Dishes

Grilled Eggplant Parmesan

Grilling gives eggplant a smoky flavor, and eliminating the frying makes this outdoor version of Eggplant Parmesan light and fresh tasting. Use freshly grated Parmesan cheese and the ripest summer tomatoes you can find for this outdoor take on the traditional dish.

PREP: 25 MINUTES   GRILL: 9 TO 12 MINUTES

1   medium-large eggplant (about 1½ pounds), cut lengthwise into 4 slices

1   tablespoon plus 1 teaspoon olive oil

½   teaspoon salt

¼   teaspoon coarsely ground black pepper

4   ounces mozzarella cheese, shredded (1 cup)

¼   cup grated Parmesan cheese

½   cup loosely packed fresh basil leaves, sliced

2   medium ripe tomatoes, each cut into 4 slices

1 Prepare grill. Lightly brush eggplant slices with oil and sprinkle with salt and pepper. In small bowl, mix mozzarella cheese, Parmesan cheese, and basil; set aside.

2 Place eggplant slices on grill over medium heat. Cook 8 to 10 minutes, until tender and lightly browned, turning once. Top eggplant slices with tomato slices and cheese mixture. Cover grill and cook 1 to 2 minutes, until cheese melts and tomato slices are warm.

Makes 4 main-dish servings

EACH SERVING: About 205 calories, 10 g protein, 15 g carbohydrate, 13 g total fat (5 g saturated), 4 g fiber, 26 mg cholesterol, 500 mg sodium

TIP
Look for an eggplant that is firm, without any soft brown spots.

Crumb-Topped Tomatoes

You can't get the crumbs crusty on the grill, so brown them ahead of time in a skillet. The crumbs may be prepared up to a day ahead and refrigerated. These would make the perfect accompaniment to Grilled Halibut with Fresh Dill (page 100) or Red-Wine & Rosemary Porterhouse (page 49).

PREP: 15 MINUTES   GRILL: 8 TO 10 MINUTES

2 tablespoons margarine or butter

1 cup fresh bread crumbs (about 2 slices firm white bread)

1 garlic clove, crushed with garlic press

2 tablespoons chopped fresh parsley leaves

½ teaspoon salt

½ teaspoon coarsely ground black pepper

8 ripe plum tomatoes

1 In 10-inch skillet, melt margarine or butter over low heat. Add bread crumbs and cook, stirring, until lightly browned. Stir in garlic; cook 30 seconds. Remove skillet from heat; stir in parsley, salt, and pepper.

2 Cut each tomato horizontally in half. Top each tomato half with some crumb mixture. Place tomatoes on grill over medium heat and cook until hot but not mushy, 8 to 10 minutes.

Makes 8 accompaniment servings

EACH SERVING: About 40 calories, 1 g protein, 3 g carbohydrate, 3 g total fat (1 g saturated), 0 g fiber, 0 mg cholesterol, 200 mg sodium

TIP
To make fresh bread crumbs, tear bread into large pieces and process the pieces to crumbs in a food processor. For dried bread crumbs, cut stale bread into large chunks and process the chunks to crumbs in a food processor. Store the crumbs in zip-tight plastic bags and freeze until needed.

Grilled Polenta with Fontina

This easy side dish begins with slices of precooked polenta from the supermarket. We added melted cheese and chopped tomatoes for a tasty topping. Precooked polenta comes in a log shape and may be found in the dairy section of your supermarket.

PREP: 10 MINUTES   GRILL: ABOUT 10 MINUTES

1 In small bowl, combine tomatoes, parsley, salt, and pepper; set aside.

2 Brush both sides of polenta slices with olive oil. Place polenta on grill over medium heat and cook 5 minutes, or until underside is golden. Turn slices and top with Fontina cheese. Cook polenta about 5 minutes longer or just until cheese melts.

3 Transfer polenta slices to platter and top with tomato mixture.

Makes 6 accompaniment servings

EACH SERVING: About 150 calories, 5 g protein, 19 g carbohydrate, 5 g total fat (2 g saturated), 3 g fiber, 11 mg cholesterol, 380 mg sodium

2 ripe medium tomatoes (about 12 ounces), chopped

2 tablespoons chopped fresh parsley leaves

¼ teaspoon salt

⅛ teaspoon coarsely ground black pepper

1 package (24 ounces) precooked polenta, cut into 12 slices

1 tablespoon olive oil

2 ounces Fontina cheese, shredded (½ cup)

TIP
Can't find Fontina? Substitute Monterey Jack or Muenster cheese. If you'd like to save time, top the grilled polenta with your favorite store-bought salsa instead of our fresh tomato topping.

Grilled Vegetables Vinaigrette

Serve these vegetables as an accompaniment to any grilled meat, poultry, or seafood. For a delightful summer salad, cut the grilled vegetables into bite-size pieces and toss them with potatoes from Lemon-Garlic Potato Packet (page 112) or from one of the other grilled potato packets.

PREP: 15 MINUTES   GRILL: 10 TO 15 MINUTES

1 Prepare Vinaigrette: In large bowl, with wire whisk, mix olive oil, vinegar, chopped tarragon, salt, pepper, and sugar. Add yellow and red peppers, zucchini, eggplant, and portobello mushrooms to bowl; toss to coat.

2 Place yellow and red peppers, zucchini, eggplant, and portobello mushrooms on grill over medium heat and cook, turning vegetables occasionally, and brushing with some of the vinaigrette remaining in bowl, until vegetables are browned and tender when pierced with a fork, 10 to 15 minutes. Once vegetables are cooked, cut each portobello in quarters to serve. Serve with remaining vinaigrette. Garnish with fresh tarragon sprigs if you like.   *Makes 8 accompaniment servings*

EACH SERVING: About 170 calories, 3 g protein, 11 g carbohydrate, 14 g total fat (2 g saturated), 2 g fiber, 0 mg cholesterol, 445 mg sodium

½ cup olive oil

½ cup white wine vinegar

8 teaspoons chopped fresh tarragon

1½ teaspoons salt

1½ teaspoons coarsely ground black pepper

1 teaspoon sugar

2 medium-size yellow peppers, halved lengthwise, seeds removed

2 medium-size red peppers, halved lengthwise, seeds removed

4 small zucchini (6 ounces each), halved lengthwise

4 baby eggplants (4 ounces each), halved lengthwise

2 medium-size portobello mushrooms (4 ounces each), stems removed

Fresh tarragon sprigs (optional)

TIP
Going to a picnic? You can grill the vegetables, toss them with the vinaigrette, and carry them along.

Campfire Corn with Herb Butter

Roasting brings out the nutty flavor of fresh corn on the cob, and leaving the husks on prevents the delicate kernels from drying out. For an added taste treat, serve the corn with wedges of lemon or lime; the tart citrus flavor complements the sweetness of the corn.

PREP: 15 MINUTES PLUS SOAKING   GRILL: 20 TO 30 MINUTES

6   medium ears corn with husks
6   (8-inch) pieces kitchen twine
1   medium shallot, minced
3   tablespoons margarine or butter, softened
2   tablespoons minced fresh parsley leaves
1   teaspoon minced fresh tarragon leaves
1   teaspoon freshly grated lemon peel
½   teaspoon salt
1⅛   teaspoons ground black pepper

1   Gently pull husks three-fourths of the way down on each ear of corn; remove silk. In large saucepot or kettle, place corn with husks, kitchen twine, and enough water to cover; let soak for at least 15 minutes. (Soaking corn with husks in water helps keep husks from burning on grill.)

2   Meanwhile, in small bowl, stir shallot, margarine or butter, parsley, tarragon, lemon peel, salt, and pepper. Let stand at room temperature, or refrigerate overnight if you like.

3   Remove corn from water; drain well. With pastry brush, brush the kernels of each ear of corn with some of the margarine mixture. Pull husks back up and, with twine, tie them at top of the ears.

4   Place corn on grill over medium heat; grill 20 to 30 minutes, turning occasionally, until husks are brown and dry and kernels are tender.

Makes 6 accompaniment servings

EACH SERVING: About 140 calories, 3 g protein, 20 g carbohydrate, 7 g total fat (1 g saturated), 3 g fiber, 0 mg cholesterol, 270 mg sodium.

TIP
Can't find shallots? Substitute finely chopped red or green onion.

Veggie Kabobs

A slightly sweet balsamic vinaigrette adds zip to an assortment of colorful vegetables. For added variety, thread large mushroom caps and wedges of red onion on the skewers with the other vegetables. Prepare extra vinaigrette and additional skewers.

PREP: 15 MINUTES   GRILL: 15 TO 20 MINUTES

3 small zucchini (about 6 ounces each), cut diagonally into 1-inch chunks

3 small yellow summer squash (about 6 ounces each), cut diagonally into 1-inch chunks

6 ripe plum tomatoes (about 1¼ pounds), each cut lengthwise in half

1 tablespoon brown sugar

1 tablespoon balsamic vinegar

½ teaspoon salt

⅛ teaspoon coarsely ground black pepper

⅛ teaspoon ground cinnamon

3 tablespoons olive oil

¾ cup loosely packed fresh basil leaves, thinly sliced

1 Onto 6 long metal skewers, alternately thread zucchini chunks, yellow squash chunks, and tomato halves, leaving about ⅛ inch space between each vegetable piece to allow even cooking. (Threading zucchini and squash through skin side gives vegetables more stability on skewers.)

2 In cup, combine brown sugar, vinegar, salt, pepper, cinnamon, and 2 tablespoons olive oil. Brush kabobs with remaining 1 tablespoon olive oil.

3 Place kabobs on grill over medium heat; cook 15 to 20 minutes, until vegetables are browned and tender. Turn kabobs occasionally and brush vegetables with some vinaigrette during last 3 minutes of cooking.

4 To serve, arrange kabobs on large platter; drizzle with any remaining vinaigrette and sprinkle with basil.   *Makes 6 accompaniment servings*

EACH SERVING: About 120 calories, 3 g protein, 13 g carbohydrate, 7 g total fat (1 g saturated), 3 g fiber, 0 mg cholesterol, 210 mg sodium

TIP
Be sure to use plum tomatoes in this recipe. They are firm, have a low moisture content, and won't fall apart when grilled.

Chili Potato Packet

We turned up the heat with ground red pepper, onion, and chili powder for
Tex-Mex appeal. To jazz it up even further, toss the grilled potatoes with cooked corn kernels, fresh lime juice,
chopped cilantro, and shredded Monterey Jack cheese.

PREP: 15 MINUTES   GRILL: 30 MINUTES

1 In large bowl, toss potatoes, red pepper, onion, olive oil, chili powder, salt, and ground red pepper until potatoes are evenly coated.

2 Layer two 30" by 18" sheets heavy-duty foil to make a double thickness. Place potato mixture on center of stacked foil. Bring short ends of foil up and over potatoes; fold several times to seal well. Fold remaining sides of foil several times to seal in juices.

3 Place packet on grill over medium heat and cook 30 minutes, or until potatoes are fork-tender, turning packet over once halfway through grilling.   *Makes about 6 cups or 8 accompaniment servings*

EACH SERVING: About 145 calories, 4 g protein, 26 g carbohydrate, 4 g total fat (1 g saturated), 3 g fiber, 0 mg cholesterol, 285 mg sodium

2½ pounds red potatoes, cut into 1-inch chunks

1 large red pepper, cut into 1-inch pieces

1 medium onion, coarsely chopped

2 tablespoons olive oil

1 tablespoon chili powder

1 teaspoon salt

¼ teaspoon ground red pepper (cayenne)

TIP
Try substituting peeled and cut sweet potatoes for the red potatoes and use a green pepper in place of the red.

Lemon-Garlic Potato Packet

Whole cloves of garlic grill up butter-soft along with the potatoes. If you'd like, once the potatoes and garlic are cooked (and while they're still warm), toss them with your favorite vinaigrette for a grilled potato salad. Tossing the potatoes with the dressing while they're warm helps them absorb the flavor.

PREP: 15 MINUTES   GRILL: 30 MINUTES

2½ pounds red potatoes, cut into 1-inch chunks

12 garlic cloves, peeled

2 tablespoons olive oil

1½ teaspoons freshly grated lemon peel

1 teaspoon salt

¼ teaspoon coarsely ground black pepper

1 In large bowl, toss potatoes, garlic, olive oil, lemon peel, salt, and pepper until potatoes are evenly coated.

2 Layer two 30" by 18" sheets heavy-duty foil to make a double thickness. Place potato mixture on center of stacked foil. Bring short ends of foil up and over potatoes; fold several times to seal well. Fold remaining sides of foil several times to seal in juices.

3 Place packet on grill over medium heat and cook 30 minutes, or until potatoes are fork-tender, turning packet over once halfway through grilling. *Makes about 6 cups or 8 accompaniment servings*

EACH SERVING: About 140 calories, 3 g protein, 25 g carbohydrate, 4 g total fat (1 g saturated), 2 g fiber, 0 mg cholesterol, 275 mg sodium

Shallot & Herb Potato Packet Prepare as above but omit garlic. Add 2 medium shallots, thinly sliced, and 2 teaspoons minced fresh thyme leaves or ½ teaspoon dried thyme. Wrap and grill as above. Sprinkle with ⅓ cup chopped fresh parsley before serving. *Makes about 6 cups or 8 accompaniment servings*

EACH SERVING: About 140 calories, 3 g protein, 25 g carbohydrate, 4 g total fat (1 g saturated), 2 g fiber, 0 mg cholesterol, 280 mg sodium

Vegetarian Burritos

Onion, peppers, and zucchini are grilled and rolled in tortillas with shredded cheeses for an all-in-one entrée.
If you prefer your burritos mild, substitute Monterey Jack without jalapeño chiles or use all Cheddar cheese.
Serve with your favorite bottled salsa and a dollop of sour cream, if you like.

PREP: 25 MINUTES   GRILL: ABOUT 20 MINUTES

1 tablespoon plus 1 teaspoon vegetable oil

1 teaspoon chili powder

1 teaspoon ground cumin

½ teaspoon salt

¼ teaspoon coarsely ground black pepper

2 medium zucchini (about 10 ounces each), cut lengthwise, ¼ inch thick

1 large onion, cut into ½-inch-thick slices

1 medium red pepper, quartered, stem and seeds discarded

1 medium green pepper, quartered, stem and seeds discarded

4 (10-inch) flour tortillas

½ cup shredded sharp Cheddar cheese (2 ounces)

½ cup shredded Monterey Jack cheese with jalapeño chiles (2 ounces)

½ cup packed fresh cilantro leaves

1 In small bowl, mix vegetable oil, chili powder, cumin, salt, and black pepper. Brush 1 side of zucchini slices, onion slices, and pepper pieces with oil mixture.

2 Place vegetables, oiled side down, on grill over medium heat, and cook 15 to 20 minutes, turning once, until tender and golden. Transfer vegetables to plate as they finish cooking.

3 Arrange one-fourth of grilled vegetables down center of each tortilla; sprinkle with Cheddar and Monterey Jack cheeses. Place open burritos on grill. Cover grill and cook 1 minute, or until cheeses melt.

4 Transfer burritos to plates. Sprinkle cilantro over cheese, then fold sides of tortillas over filling. Serve with salsa if you like.

Makes 4 main-dish servings

EACH SERVING: About 330 calories, 11 g protein, 43 g carbohydrate, 14 g total fat (4 g saturated), 4 g fiber, 15 mg cholesterol, 655 mg sodium

TIP
Burritos may be cut into bite-size portions and served as appetizers.

Glazed Japanese Eggplant

Make sure you buy Japanese eggplants for this recipe—they're purple and usually long and slender. Delicious either hot off the grill, chilled, or at room temperature. For an added touch, sprinkle the eggplants with toasted sesame seeds just before serving.

PREP: 15 MINUTES   GRILL: ABOUT 10 MINUTES

1 With knife, score cut side of each eggplant half with several ¼-inch-deep parallel diagonal slits, being careful not to cut all the way through to skin. Repeat with a second set of slits perpendicular to the first to form a diamond pattern.

2 In small bowl, with fork, mix brown sugar, ginger, soy sauce, vinegar, sesame oil, cornstarch, garlic, and 3 tablespoons water.

3 Brush cut side of eggplant halves with vegetable oil. With tongs, place eggplant halves on grill, cut side down, over medium heat. Grill eggplant 5 minutes, or until lightly browned.

4 Fold 34" by 18" sheet of heavy-duty foil crosswise in half. Place eggplant halves on double thickness of foil. Pour soy-sauce mixture over eggplant halves, bring long sides of foil up, and fold several times to seal well. Fold over ends to seal in juices.

5 Place foil packet on grill over medium heat, and cook 5 minutes, or until eggplant is soft. To serve, open packet, lift out eggplant and spoon any juices over.   *Makes 6 accompaniment servings*

EACH SERVING: About 85 calories, 2 g protein, 13 g carbohydrate, 4 g total fat (0 g saturated), 2 g fiber, 0 mg cholesterol, 570 mg sodium

6 medium Japanese eggplants (about 5 ounces each), each cut lengthwise in half

1 tablespoon dark brown sugar

1 tablespoon minced peeled fresh ginger

3 tablespoons soy sauce

1 tablespoon seasoned rice vinegar

½ teaspoon Asian sesame oil

¼ teaspoon cornstarch

3 garlic cloves, crushed with garlic press

4 teaspoons vegetable oil

TIP
Seasoned rice vinegar contains both salt and a sweetener. It makes a delicious, nonfat addition to salad dressings, coleslaws, chicken and pork marinades, and barbecue sauces.

Chiles Relleños

If you prefer hotter flavor: After grilling and before filling the chiles, remove the seeds and veins but don't rinse the insides. Serve the chiles with salsa, if you like, but be aware that poblanos can sometimes be very hot; so choose your salsa accordingly. If you have access to a Latin American market, look for Queso Blanco and use it in place of the Monterey Jack.

PREP: 20 MINUTES   GRILL: ABOUT 25 MINUTES

6 medium poblano chiles (about 4 ounces each)

6 ounces Monterey Jack cheese, shredded (1½ cups)

1 cup corn kernels cut from cobs (about 2 medium ears)

½ cup loosely packed fresh cilantro leaves, chopped

1 Place whole poblano chiles on grill over medium heat and cook, turning occasionally, until blistered and blackened on all sides, 10 to 15 minutes.

2 Transfer chiles to large sheet of foil. Wrap foil around chiles and allow to steam at room temperature 15 minutes, or until cool enough to handle.

3 Meanwhile, in medium bowl, combine cheese, corn, and cilantro.

4 Remove chiles from foil. Cut 2-inch lengthwise slit in side of each chile, being careful not to cut through top or bottom. Under cold running water, gently peel off skin. Remove seeds and veins from opening; rinse with running water. Pat chiles dry with paper towels.

5 With spoon, fill each chile with about ½ cup cheese mixture. Gently reshape chiles to close opening. Place 3 filled chiles in single layer on each of two 18" by 18" sheets of heavy-duty foil. Bring 2 sides of foil up and fold several times to seal well. Fold over ends to seal in juices. (Recipe can be prepared to this point and refrigerated up to 6 hours before grilling.)

6 Place foil packet on grill over medium heat and cook 10 minutes to heat chiles and melt cheese.   *Makes 6 accompaniment servings*

EACH SERVING: About 160 calories, 9 g protein, 13 g carbohydrate, 9 g total fat (5 g saturated), 2 g fiber, 30 mg cholesterol, 160 mg sodium

TIP
For a great brunch dish, add half a cup of minced ham to the corn mixture, then cook as directed.

Mediterranean Grilled Eggplant & Summer Squash

This recipe doubles easily—if you're feeding a crowd, grill the vegetables in batches.

PREP: 15 MINUTES   GRILL: 15 MINUTES

3   tablespoons olive oil

2   tablespoons red wine vinegar

2   teaspoons Dijon mustard

¼   teaspoon salt

¼   teaspoon coarsely ground black pepper

1   garlic clove, crushed with garlic press

1   medium zucchini (about 8 ounces), cut lengthwise into ¼-inch-thick slices

1   medium yellow squash (about 8 ounces), cut lengthwise into ¼-inch-thick slices

1   small eggplant (about 1¼ pounds), cut lengthwise into ¼-inch-thick slices

2   tablespoons chopped fresh mint leaves

1   ounce crumbled ricotta salata* or feta cheese (¼ cup)

*Ricotta salata is a firm, white, lightly salted cheese made from sheep's milk. Look for it in supermarkets, cheese shops, and Italian groceries.

1 Prepare vinaigrette: In small bowl, with wire whisk, mix olive oil, vinegar, mustard, salt, pepper, and garlic.

2 Brush 1 side of each vegetable slice with some of the vinaigrette. Place vegetables on grill over medium heat and cook, turning once and brushing with remaining vinaigrette, until vegetables are browned and tender, 10 to 15 minutes.

3 Transfer vegetables to large platter as they are done. Sprinkle with mint and ricotta salata.   *Makes 6 accompaniment servings*

EACH SERVING: About 115 calories, 3 g protein, 9 g carbohydrate, 8 g total fat (2 g saturated), 2 g fiber, 4 mg cholesterol, 220 mg sodium

TIP
Grilled vegetables make a wonderful sandwich. Fill sliced crusty Italian bread with vegetables and extra cheese.

Sauces, Rubs & Salsas

Lime-Herb Rub

PREP: 15 MINUTES
MAKES: ABOUT 1½ CUPS

Use this for our Mixed Grill with Asian Flavors (page 65). It's also great rubbed under the skin of a chicken or over a pork tenderloin.

2 limes
2 cups loosely packed fresh cilantro
    leaves, chopped
2 cups loosely packed fresh mint leaves,
    chopped
2 tablespoons brown sugar
2 tablespoons minced peeled fresh
    ginger
3 garlic cloves, crushed with garlic press
2 green onions, thinly sliced
2 teaspoons salt
1 teaspoon crushed red pepper

From limes, grate 1 tablespoon peel and squeeze 2 tablespoons juice. Combine lime peel, lime juice, cilantro, mint, brown sugar, ginger, garlic, green onions, salt, and crushed red pepper.

EACH ⅓ CUP SERVING: ABOUT 70 CALORIES, 3 G PROTEIN, 16 G CARBOHYDRATE, 1 G TOTAL FAT (0 G SATURATED), 6 G FIBER, 0 MG CHOLESTEROL, 1,195 MG SODIUM

Mango Salsa

PREP: 15 MINUTES
MAKES: ABOUT 4 CUPS

The combination of mango and kiwifruit gives this salsa its sweet and tangy flavor . Try substituting chopped pitted fresh cherries and a diced yellow pepper for the mango and kiwifruit.

2 ripe medium mangoes, peeled and
    coarsely chopped
2 medium kiwifruit, peeled and coarsely
    chopped
3 tablespoons seasoned rice vinegar
1 tablespoon grated peeled fresh ginger
1 tablespoon minced fresh cilantro
    leaves

In medium bowl, combine mangoes, kiwifruit, rice vinegar, ginger, and cilantro. Cover and refrigerate if not serving right away.

EACH ¼ CUP SERVING: ABOUT 25 CALORIES, 0 G PROTEIN, 6 G CARBOHYDRATE, 0 G TOTAL FAT (0 G SATURATED), 1 G FIBER, 0 MG CHOLESTEROL, 60 MG SODIUM

Spicy Peppercorn Rub

PREP: 10 MINUTES
MAKES: ABOUT ½ CUP

Our simple salt-free blend works well for steak, pork, chicken, or lamb. We like to pat about 2 tablespoons on a 1- to 2-pound steak—you can use more or less, depending on the meat's thickness.

3 tablespoons coriander seeds
3 tablespoons cumin seeds
3 tablespoons fennel seeds
1 tablespoon whole black peppercorns

Place all ingredients in zip-tight plastic bag. Place kitchen towel over bag and, with meat mallet or rolling pin, coarsely crush spices. Rub desired amount all over steak(s) before grilling. If not using right away, store rub in tightly sealed container in cool, dry place up to 2 months.

EACH TABLESPOON: ABOUT 25 CALORIES, 2 G PROTEIN, 4 G CARBOHYDRATE, 1 G TOTAL FAT (0 G SATURATED), 2 G FIBER, 0 MG CHOLESTEROL, 7 MG SODIUM

Chunky BBQ Sauce

PREP: 10 MINUTES
COOK: 25 MINUTES
MAKES: ABOUT 4 CUPS

Good on pork or chicken. Refrigerate up to 1 week or freeze up to 2 months.

1 tablespoon vegetable oil
1 large onion, diced
3 garlic cloves, minced
2 tablespoons minced peeled fresh
  ginger
1 teaspoon ground cumin
1 can (14½ ounces) tomatoes in puree,
  chopped, puree reserved
1 bottle (12 ounces) chili sauce
⅓ cup cider vinegar
2 tablespoons brown sugar
2 tablespoons light (mild) molasses
2 teaspoons dry mustard
1 tablespoon cornstarch

1 In 12-inch skillet, heat oil over medium heat until hot. Add onion and cook 10 minutes, or until tender, stirring occasionally. Add garlic and ginger and cook 1 minute, stirring. Stir in cumin.

2 Stir in tomatoes, reserved puree, chili sauce, vinegar, brown sugar, molasses, and dry mustard; heat to boiling over high heat. Reduce to medium-high and cook, uncovered, 5 minutes, stirring occasionally.

3 In cup, mix cornstarch with 2 tablespoons water until blended. Stir into sauce mixture and cook 1 to 2 minutes longer, until sauce boils and thickens. Cover and refrigerate if not using right away.

EACH ½ CUP: ABOUT 120 CALORIES, 2 G PROTEIN, 25 G CARBOHYDRATE, 2 G TOTAL FAT (0 G SATURATED), 1 G FIBER, 0 MG CHOLESTEROL, 655 MG SODIUM

Salt-Free Herb Rub

PREP: 5 MINUTES
MAKES: ABOUT ¼ CUP

Our crush of dried herbs may earn your saltshaker a well-deserved summer vacation. Try it on grilled pork or fish.

2 tablespoons dried rosemary
2 tablespoons dried thyme
1 tablespoon dried tarragon
1 tablespoon coarsely ground black
  pepper

In mortar with pestle, or with fingers, crush together rosemary, thyme, tarragon, and pepper. Use 2 teaspoons herb mixture per pound of uncooked beef or pork; 1 teaspoon per pound of uncooked fish or chicken. Store in tightly covered container and use within 6 months.

EACH TEASPOON: ABOUT 5 CALORIES, 0 G PROTEIN, 1 G CARBOHYDRATE, 0 G TOTAL FAT (0 G SATURATED), 0 G FIBER, 0 MG CHOLESTEROL, 1 MG SODIUM

Soy Marinade

PREP: 10 MINUTES
MAKES: ABOUT ¾ CUP

⅓ cup soy sauce
3 tablespoons seasoned rice vinegar
2 tablespoons packed brown sugar
2 tablespoons minced peeled fresh
  ginger
1 tablespoon vegetable oil
2 garlic cloves, crushed with garlic press
2 green onions, thinly sliced
½ teaspoon Asian sesame oil
¼ teaspoon crushed red pepper

In a medium bowl, stir together soy sauce, vinegar, brown sugar, ginger, vegetable oil, garlic, green onions, sesame oil, and crushed red pepper. Use for chicken or pork.

EACH TABLESPOON: ABOUT 30 CALORIES, 1 G PROTEIN, 4 G CARBOHYDRATE, 1 G TOTAL FAT (0 G SATURATED), 0 G FIBER, 0 MG CHOLESTEROL, 530 MG SODIUM

Secret-Recipe BBQ Sauce

PREP:15 MINUTES
COOK: 40 MINUTES
MAKES: ABOUT 5 CUPS

Brush this mixture over anything from hamburgers to chicken.

1 tablespoon olive oil
1 large onion (12 ounces), chopped
2 tablespoons chopped peeled fresh
   ginger
3 tablespoons chili powder
3 garlic cloves, crushed with garlic press
1 can (8 ounces) crushed pineapple in
   juice
1 can (28 ounces) crushed tomatoes in
   puree
⅓ cup ketchup
¼ cup cider vinegar
3 tablespoons dark brown sugar
3 tablespoons light (mild) molasses
2 teaspoons dry mustard
1 teaspoon salt

1 In 5- to 6-quart saucepot, heat olive oil over medium heat until hot. (Do not use a smaller pan; sauce bubbles up and splatters during cooking—the deeper the pan, the better.) Add onion and ginger, and cook 10 minutes, or until onion is tender and golden. Add chili powder; cook 1 minute, stirring. Add garlic and crushed pineapple with its juice, and cook 1 minute longer.

2 Remove from heat. Stir in tomatoes with their puree, ketchup, vinegar, brown sugar, molasses, dry mustard, and salt.

3 Spoon one-fourth of sauce into blender. At low speed, blend until smooth. Pour sauce into bowl; repeat with remaining sauce. Return sauce to saucepot; heat to boiling over high heat. Reduce heat to medium-low and cook, partially covered, 25 minutes or until reduced to about 5 cups, stirring occasionally.

4 Cover and refrigerate if not using right away. Sauce will keep up to 1 week in refrigerator or up to 2 months in freezer.

EACH CUP: ABOUT 220 CALORIES, 3 G PROTEIN, 47 G CARBOHYDRATE, 3 G TOTAL FAT (0 G SATURATED), 4 G FIBER, 0 MG CHOLESTEROL, 960 MG SODIUM

Cucumber Relish

PREP:10 MINUTES
MAKES: ABOUT 2½ CUPS

Delicious with our Chicken & Beef Saté (page 43) or served alongside grilled fish.

4 medium Kirby cucumbers (about 4
   ounces each), diced
¼ cup seasoned rice vinegar
2 tablespoons diced red onion
1 tablespoon vegetable oil
¼ teaspoon crushed red pepper

In medium bowl, with spoon, combine cucumber, vinegar, red onion, vegetable oil, and crushed red pepper. Cover and refrigerate until ready to serve.

EACH ¼ CUP SERVING: ABOUT 25 CALORIES, 0 G PROTEIN, 3 G CARBOHYDRATE, 1 G TOTAL FAT (0 G SATURATED), 0 G FIBER, 0 MG CHOLESTEROL, 120 MG SODIUM

Chimichurri Sauce

PREP: 15 MINUTES
MAKES: ABOUT ½ CUP

This tasty green sauce, thick with fresh herbs, is as common in Argentina as ketchup is in the United States. It can be prepared ahead and refrigerated up to 2 days. Great drizzled over meat and poultry—or tossed with hot cooked pasta. You can even use it as a salad dressing.

1½ cups loosely packed fresh parsley leaves, finely chopped
1½ cups loosely packed fresh cilantro leaves, finely chopped
¼ cup olive oil
3 tablespoons red wine vinegar
1 garlic clove, crushed with garlic press
¼ teaspoon coarsely ground black pepper
¼ teaspoon salt

In small bowl, mix parsley, cilantro, olive oil, vinegar, garlic, pepper, and salt. Cover and refrigerate if not using right away.

EACH TABLESPOON: ABOUT 65 CALORIES, 0 G PROTEIN, 1 G CARBOHYDRATE, 7 G TOTAL FAT (1 G SATURATED), 0 G FIBER, 0 MG CHOLESTEROL, 70 MG SODIUM

Guacamole

PREP: 20 MINUTES
MAKES: ABOUT 3 CUPS

Great with Steak Fajitas with Guacamole (page 57), grilled pork, or grilled chicken, or as a topper for Grilled Flatbread (page 13).

2 medium ripe avocados (about 8 ounces each), peeled and cut into 1-inch chunks
2 ripe medium tomatoes, coarsely chopped
1 jalapeño chile, seeded and minced
1 cup loosely packed fresh cilantro leaves, chopped
1 tablespoon fresh lime juice
½ teaspoon salt

In medium bowl, gently stir avocados, tomatoes, jalapeño, cilantro, lime juice, and salt. Cover with plastic wrap and refrigerate if not serving right away.

EACH TABLESPOON: ABOUT 15 CALORIES, 0 G PROTEIN, 1 G CARBOHYDRATE, 1 G TOTAL FAT (0 G SATURATED), 0 G FIBER, 0 MG CHOLESTEROL, 25 MG SODIUM

Pineapple Salsa

PREP: 15 MINUTES
MAKES: ABOUT 4 CUPS

2 limes
1 ripe pineapple (rind removed), cored and coarsely chopped
1 cup loosely packed fresh cilantro leaves, chopped
1 jalapeño chile, seeded and minced
1 green onion, sliced
1 teaspoon sugar
¼ teaspoon salt
⅛ teaspoon coarsely ground black pepper

From limes, grate ½ teaspoon peel and squeeze 2 tablespoons juice. In medium bowl, mix lime peel and juice with pineapple, cilantro, jalapeño, green onion, sugar, salt, and pepper. Cover and refrigerate until ready to serve.

EACH ¼ CUP SERVING: ABOUT 20 CALORIES, 0 G PROTEIN, 5 G CARBOHYDRATE, 0 G TOTAL FAT, 1 G FIBER, 0 MG CHOLESTEROL, 35 MG SODIUM

Creamy Peanut Dipping Sauce

PREP: 20 MINUTES
COOK: 5 MINUTES
MAKES: ABOUT 2¼ CUPS

Serve this sauce with our Mixed Grill with Asian Flavors (page 65), use it as a dressing for a crunchy slaw, or toss it with hot cooked linguine and serve at room temperature or chilled.

¾ cup creamy peanut butter
¼ cup boiling water
¾ cup well-stirred unsweetened light coconut milk (not cream of coconut)
½ cup packed fresh cilantro leaves, chopped
2 tablespoons packed brown sugar
2 tablespoons soy sauce
5 teaspoons seasoned rice vinegar
½ teaspoon crushed red pepper
1 small garlic clove, crushed with garlic press

In medium bowl, with wire whisk, mix peanut butter and boiling water until blended, Stir in coconut milk, cilantro, brown sugar, soy sauce, vinegar, crushed red pepper, and garlic until combined. Refrigerate sauce until ready to serve. Let stand at room temperature 30 minutes before serving to allow flavors to develop.

EACH TABLESPOON: ABOUT 40 CALORIES, 1 G PROTEIN, 2 G CARBOHYDRATE, 3 G TOTAL FAT (1 G SATURATED), 0 G FIBER, 0 MG CHOLESTEROL, 100 MG SODIUM

French Tarragon Rub

PREP: 10 MINUTES
MAKES: ⅓ CUP

This delicious rub has all the flavor but none of the fat of a rich béarnaise sauce.

2 medium shallots, minced (¼ cup)
2 tablespoons red wine vinegar
1 tablespoon dried tarragon
1 teaspoon salt
½ teaspoon coarsely ground black pepper

In cup, stir together shallots, vinegar, tarragon, salt, and pepper. Rub full amount all over meat or chicken before grilling.

EACH BATCH: ABOUT 50 CALORIES, 2 G PROTEIN, 11 G CARBOHYDRATE, 0 G TOTAL FAT (0 G SATURATED), 1 G FIBER, 0 MG CHOLESTEROL, 2,340 MG SODIUM

Horseradish Salsa

PREP: 15 MINUTES
MAKES: 2 CUPS

For a peppier salsa, add more horseradish.

3 ripe medium tomatoes (about 1 pound), cut into ½-inch dice
1 cup loosely packed fresh parsley leaves, chopped
½ small red onion, minced
2 tablespoons bottled white horseradish
1 tablespoon balsamic vinegar
1 tablespoon olive oil
½ teaspoon salt

In medium bowl, combine tomatoes, parsley, red onion, horseradish, vinegar, olive oil, and salt. Cover and refrigerate until serving time.

EACH ¼ CUP SERVING: ABOUT 35 CALORIES, 1 G PROTEIN, 4 G CARBOHYDRATE, 2 G TOTAL FAT (0 G SATURATED), 1 G FIBER, 0 MG CHOLESTEROL, 180 MG SODIUM

Index

METRIC CONVERSIONS

LENGTH

If you know:	Multiply by:	To find:
INCHES	25.0	MILLIMETERS
INCHES	2.5	CENTIMETERS
FEET	30.0	CENTIMETERS
YARDS	0.9	METERS
MILES	1.6	KILOMETERS
MILLIMETERS	0.04	INCHES
CENTIMETERS	0.4	INCHES
METERS	3.3	FEET
METERS	1.1	YARDS
KILOMETERS	0.6	MILES

VOLUME

If you know:	Multiply by:	To find:
TEASPOONS	5.0	MILLILITERS
TABLESPOONS	15.0	MILLILITERS
FLUID OUNCES	30.0	MILLILITERS
CUPS	0.24	LITERS
PINTS	0.47	LITERS
QUARTS	0.95	LITERS
GALLONS	3.8	LITERS
MILLILITERS	0.03	FLUID OUNCES
LITERS	4.2	CUPS
LITERS	2.1	PINTS
LITERS	1.06	QUARTS
LITERS	0.26	GALLONS

WEIGHT

If you know:	Multiply by:	To find:
OUNCES	28.0	GRAMS
POUNDS	0.45	KILOGRAMS
GRAMS	0.035	OUNCES
KILOGRAMS	2.2	POUNDS

TEMPERATURE

If you know:	Multiply by:	To find:
DEGREES FAHRENHEIT	0.56 (AFTER SUBTRACTING 32)	DEGREES CELSIUS
DEGREES CELSIUS	1.8 (THEN ADD 32)	DEGREES FAHRENHEIT